Down and Out
in Providence

Down and Out in Providence

Memoir of a
Homeless Bishop

Geralyn Wolf

*To Beverley Myers
with God's blessings.*

+ Geralyn Wolf

A Crossroad Book
The Crossroad Publishing Company
New York

The Crossroad Publishing Company
16 Penn Plaza, 481 Eighth Avenue
New York, NY 10001

Printed in the United States of America

This text of this book is set in 11/16 Palatino.
The display faces are Mona Lisa Solid and Lettres Éclatées.

Library of Congress Cataloging-in-Publication Data

Wolf, Geralyn.
    Down and out in Providence : memoir of a homeless Bishop / Geralyn Wolf.
        p. cm.
    Includes bibliographical references.
    ISBN 0-8245-2276-1 (alk. paper)
    1. Church work with the homeless. 2. Helping behavior – Religious aspects – Christianity. 3. Social work with the homeless. 4. Caring – Religious aspects – Christianity. 5. Compassion – Religious aspects – Christianity. 6. Wolf, Geralyn. I. Title.

BV4456.W65 2005
261.8'325'092 – dc22

                                                              2005003091

1 2 3 4 5 6 7 8 9 10   10 09 08 07 06 05

In thanksgiving
for my mother and father,
who gave me a home,
and Valerie and Barbara,
with whom I shared it

CONTENTS

PROLOGUE

She was dancing — eyes closed, head tilted back, arms slowly weaving over her head as she turned. Her hair was flowing free as she lowered her arms to the height of her shoulders; the palms of her hands opened; waiting, giving, receiving.

Elizabeth was dancing as if nobody was watching. But I was. I had gone out to get some milk for my houseguest, and before I opened the door, I looked in the window.

For a glorious moment, I was with her, my eyes closed, a gentle smile on my lips, a sense of utter freedom. It all ended when I turned the key in the door. "Good morning, Elizabeth," I happily announced. The moment was broken, but the memory endured, the memory of such self-abandonment, of dancing as if nobody was watching.

I live a very hectic and full life as the bishop of the Episcopal Diocese of Rhode Island. My secretary coordinates a busy schedule of meetings, appointments, official parish visitations, telephone calls, mail, invitations to be considered, clergy and staff concerns, diocesan events, national church responsibilities, and on and on. My day off is Monday, barely enough time to catch my breath and do some errands.

I am reflective by nature. So weaving through this active life are always the deeper questions, the challenges of trying to live a life of faith, release creativity, satisfy the contemplative heart, appease the yearning for things yet unknown that are nestled somewhere deep inside, hidden, yet present in mysterious and indefinable longings.

In 2001, when I began to plan for a four-month sabbatical, I embarked on a pilgrimage of my soul. I yearned for clarity in a life that was filled with the conflicting expectations of others, uplifted with great devotion and affection from my flock, yet shadowed by unhealthy projections and grumbling. Moments of extraordinary grace and wisdom run parallel with misjudgment and things left undone.

I yearned for a raw and bawdy truth, filled with passion and energy. Like the truth I experienced at St. Mary's in Philadelphia, where I was the vicar for six years. The soup kitchen and neighborhood were alive with the earthy banter of street life. Lovin' and cussin' went hand in hand, as did profound need and generosity. Many guests of the soup kitchen were local, neighborhood people. Others lived in shelters, in boarded-up houses, in empty lots, on steam grates, and on sidewalks. Three hundred people sat down in our soup kitchen and were served hearty homemade soup, sandwiches, and dessert with coffee or tea. Our doors opened in 1981. In 1982 we added a thrift shop, and a year later we opened a small food cooperative.

I had learned years ago of the horrible legislative actions and systemic realities that continue to jeopardize the lives of the poor and those who live on the margins. All rhetoric to the contrary, the United States has a *classism* that we fear to address.

Part of me has always felt homeless. By the time I graduated from high school, I had attended eleven schools and lived in about thirteen or fourteen houses and apartments. We weren't a military family, just on the move. Perhaps in an unconscious way, I wanted to come to terms with my own homelessness. I wanted to understand it. As I planned for a sabbatical, I recognized that the call to pilgrimage, to journey, was a call to choose to be homeless.

I shared these thoughts with Anne Nolan, the director of Crossroads in Providence, Rhode Island, an agency that helps the homeless who have medical, employment, and housing needs. I soon learned that Anne was one of those extraordinary persons who could be decisive, sensitive, wise, strong, and tearful all in the same conversation. I knew from our first visit that ours would be a good and mutually supportive relationship.

Together with Noreen Shawcross, the director of the Coalition for the Homeless, we discussed such issues as my safety, clothing, health, and length of experience ("If it's only a few days, don't worry; you will already be helpful to the cause of the homeless"). We agreed on a one-month period. Thankfully, they did not try to describe the experience, the staff's role, or the personal lives of their homeless clients. Because of my previous health problems, Anne and Noreen suggested that I return home if I became sick. This was good advice. After my third night on the street, I went home with a fever one evening. Thankfully, I was well by the next morning.

I entered homelessness with very little knowledge of what to expect. However, I never pretended to myself that I was really homeless. After all, I entered Crossroads from a warm and comfortable home, to which I would return. I never underestimated the sheer sense of fear and desperation with which most entered into a state of homelessness.

I also chose to limit myself to two hundred dollars for the month, less money than some had, more than others had. I got the money from the bank, put most of it in the bottom of my boots, between the insert and the sole, keeping about five dollars in my pocket. I had a few bus tickets that enabled me to expand my experience by staying in shelters in New York and Philadelphia.

In the midst of my pilgrimage, I stayed in seven different shelters, ate in eight meal sites other than shelters or Crossroads, and attended ten church services in five denominations, including the Episcopal Church.

Most nights I slept at Welcome Arthur, a shelter run by a nonprofit organization. The guards awakened us at 6 a.m., and a Welcome Arthur bus, called "the Goose," took us to Amos House for breakfast. Amos House also serves dinner and is another source of assistance for those in need. From there we went by foot or city bus to Crossroads, where we could stay until 6 p.m. Most took the 5 p.m. Goose back to Welcome Arthur. Once at the night shelter, we registered, had our one allowable bag checked for drugs, alcohol, or food, and went upstairs. We received a small hand towel, and we were given one sheet after we had taken a cool shower. One utility blanket was left on the bed, and there were no pillows. In the morning we followed the usual routine, leaving at 6:30 a.m. to go for breakfast.

Crossroads, where we stayed during the day, is not a shelter but a place for community. It's not a place so much for dropping in as for putting life's pieces back together. With the help of social workers and others, medical, employment, and housing needs are addressed. As with most nonprofit agencies, Crossroads is woefully understaffed for the challenges it faces.

To protect my anonymity, I had let my hair grow for the year since my idea was conceived, and I dyed it a dark brown with a temporary dye. I went to several department stores to prepare for my "new look." One young, slim, beautiful woman tried to respond to my makeup requests. I instructed her to choose a lipstick not appropriate for my skin color, and then asked her to give me full lips. Subtlety was not my goal. We had to negotiate for a really full look. When the young woman who was helping me thought I wasn't looking, she glanced at another makeup artist and rolled her eyes.

In one store, the saleswoman actually enjoyed the process of creating a full pair of lips. When she had finished, I told her that sixteen dollars was too much to pay for lipstick. Making sure no one was watching, she gave me a sample of the color and advised me to go to the drugstore.

It was important for me to maintain anonymity so I would be treated like other homeless people. I'm quite recognizable in Providence and initially considered going to a different city. However, Providence is the largest city in the diocese and state in which I serve, and I take the importance of place and ministry very seriously.

I carried a small backpack that held one sleeping bag liner, a few toiletries, one change of long underwear, two changes of regular underwear and socks, and a few odds and ends. When you carry everything, you have to travel light. Many homeless people that I met had the use of a small closet or shelf in someone's house to store some things. A few had storage garages, rented after they could no longer afford to pay the rent for their apartments. Even one relatively light bag is difficult for most to manage. Bus drivers complain about the size of various bags and the amount of time it takes to board the bus with them. As one of my friends in the shelter said, "They ain't never said anything to the shoppers during Christmas."

Many people living in the shelters had full or part-time jobs, but they did not earn enough to rent an apartment or even a room. Others were physically handicapped. Two of the men in our group were blind. Others were emotionally handicapped. Some people had lost their jobs because of the economic turn-down. More than a few could not afford recent rent increases imposed by landlords, or the rising cost of heating oil.

The community room at Crossroads served as a daytime shelter from the cold. Just as important, it served as a place where community, conversation, and family flourished. There were no exterior windows in the seventy-five-by-thirty-five-foot room where as many as 150 people gathered. Yet there was a vulnerability of spirit that allowed me to peer into windows of souls and for my soul to be revealed.

Prologue

This book is about those glances, words, and actions that revealed both humor and tragedy. All races, all types, and all conditions of people who seek their daily bread may sit in the community room. Good people. Gifted people. You. Me. All of us who are willing to admit to our hunger and to the wandering spirit that dwells within. This story is about people I love.

A Journal of Days

A NEW IDENTITY?

December 30, 2002

His eyes are rolling. Really rolling, back and forth. Hands tight against his head, holding the headphones tight against his ears. "There's seven seconds on the clock," he yells in his deep bass voice. He's a play-by-play expert. "It's tied! It's overcome! We're gonna win this motha f—a!" "It all depends on the coin toss," says a man leaning forward, excitedly, on his chair. "If we get it, we win!" "Hey," Carl shouts, "New England got the ball!"

"If we was at home we'd win," says the woman at the next table. "We is at home," says the expert. Everyone has an opinion, a play. The expert goes to the corner of the room so he can hear better. He shouts out the results, our own Howard Cosell.

"Green Bay's gonna win cause I bet on them," another woman says in a cocky confident way. "Shut up, we're playin' Miami!" says Carl, listening intently. "Hey, Carl, you still listenen' to the game?" The question is shouted from the far end of the room. "Yeah, it's a tie." "Really?" the man calls out. Carl, not wanting to be interrupted shouts back, "Hell, where you been?" "Twenty-five yards, first down!" yells Cosell. "He's gonna kick a field goal, just wait." A small woman ambles in and announces to no one in particular, "It's Miami against the Peckers." "No it ain't." says Carl in exasperation. "It's Miami and the Patriots." He gives out a shout, swivels his robust rear end, and says, "The New England Patriots are the division champions!"

Jim, a security guard at Crossroads, walks into the community room, rolling from side to side on his well-worn black sneakers, and everyone quiets down. "Everybody begin to get your things together; the bus will come in twenty minutes, in front of Johnson and Wales." I learned that the bus that comes at 5 p.m. every day is called "the Goose." The bags are packed, have been all day, put alongside the room. People slowly leave their chairs, put on coats and jackets, and drag the bags to their seats. In another ten minutes about thirty people walk down the street to the bus stop. One bag apiece, that's what the shelter says. First we stop at the Urban League Building to register. Everybody gets off the bus; women always first. I sign my name "Aly Wolf" and join everyone else in returning to the bus. About ten minutes later we turn into the prison facility in Warwick. Welcome Arthur, the shelter, is located in one of the buildings on the prison's property. "I'm talkin' to you," snaps the registrar, as I stare at the children eating dinner. The person in front of me turns and says, "She's talkin' to you!" "Come over here and register." All of a sudden a wave of fear sweeps over me; is this when they ask for an ID? I feel my wallet in my pocket; safely tucked inside is the ID we made at the office: Aly Wolf, one-time employee of the Diocese of Rhode Island, picture ID, signed by my assistant at the diocesan office, put together by me, laminated, and stamped with the diocesan seal. "What's your name?" she says. "Aly Wolf." She writes it on the page and lets me go through. Third floor, room 303, bed 2. "Hurry up, put your things down; it's time for dinner." Ravioli and green beans. I take about two minutes to eat. Then we all go back to our rooms, and we are given a small hand towel. In turn, twenty-seven women wait to use the three showers. Only then are we given one sheet to make our bed. It's only about 7:30, and there's nothing to do. The woman in bed 6 plays solitaire on a small computer she bought for under ten dollars. Across the hall they watch TV and talk as if they are twenty feet apart. "Bed 2," the matron calls, "you have to go down and sign in." Oh, no. I thought that I had made it. I put on my boots, clutching my wallet as if to add extra blessing on my ID. The registrar asks a lot of questions: Highest level of education. "One year of college," I answer. Address: 275 North Sims Street. Most recent date of employment: Dec. 23, 2002. Income: None. Reason for being in shelter: No income. First time in shelter: Yes. Divorced, no children, husband gambled some in Philadelphia; we lost everything. "Sign here please, and here, and at the two X's." That was it. No ID requested. I had to make up answers quickly. I was disturbed by how easy it was for me to lie; it almost seemed natural. Maybe it wasn't so much "lying" as starting to believe in the story I'd spent weeks fabricating.

⌒

Now the women in the shower room are talking about menopause. They're trading symptoms and advice. "Don't worry about it, you're just changing." "But," said one, "you can still get pregnant. Don't let no one tell ya you is free of that."

It's 4:45 a.m., the matron wakes the woman in bed 3, and I wake up too. Strip the bed; take the linens to the first floor. The sign on the wall reads

"Effective December 14, only one bag per person." Another bulletin board says something about our spiritual lives and attempts to touch on our hopes for the future. I read the board. The spiritual tips. Some of them are good; others seem impossible. I'd like to write some of the ideas down, but I know that there's no time.

A lot of people were raised with a church but don't attend anymore. They are spiritual. They believe in God, pray earnestly, and believe that with his help life will get better. "But I done bad things, and I'm all f—ed up."

I wonder what kind of church would provide the shelter and security for a person on the streets. Some churches offer "oppressive hospitality" too much, too soon, too overbearing, and it ends as quickly as it began. It's always difficult to find the line between respectful distance and helpful attention.

Yes, there are some good suggestions on the spiritual list. God created me. I am special. There is hope. Say no to drugs, et cetera.

"Miss," the guard says in an authoritative tone, "either you leave the building or go upstairs." I am awakened from my musings, nod and turn, and return to the third floor.

There's no point in trying to go back to sleep, because it's almost time to wake up and go to the bus. Women get dressed quickly here; there's no reason to dawdle. By 7 a.m. we'll be at Amos House for breakfast, and then walk to Crossroads for the day.

LEARNING THE ROPES

December 31, 2002

I miss lunch at Crossroads and walk a long way to St. Anthony's House on Rhodes Street. Everyone said it was just a couple of blocks away, but it is at least a mile and a half. It is worth it, though. The house was a private home at one time, complete with small parlors, a kitchen, and a dining room. I sit down to a large, hot portion of meat, potatoes, and other vegetables. Everyone is very quiet, minding their own business, looking at their plates. There is a large, white frosted cake in the middle of the table, but I never get to it.

"Stop f—in' my woman," shouts one of the diners.

"I ain't f—in' your woman."

"You heard me! Stop f—in' my woman."

"I ain't f—in' your woman."

The two men move closer together, and Bill puts his hand on what looked like a big blue mug or vase resting on the sideboard.

"I told you," he says, "stop f—in' my wife." With that he smashes the vase against the side of Charlie's face and pushes him into an old wooden china cabinet that is fastened to the wall. The glass smashes. Blood is everywhere. A woman with a red sweatshirt gets in the middle and gets kicked in the leg. The whole thing is getting out of control, but other guys break it up. I quietly finish my lunch. Outside, Charlie's face is bleeding. "You need stitches, Charlie," a woman says. "I ain't gettin' stitches. I can handle it."

I go to catch a bus back to Crossroads. I'm tired.

So many good people here. Caring about one another, carrying burdens. "I had a nervous breakdown, lost everything," says Sue. "Been off of drugs and alcohol one month. I don't want the kid remembering her grandmother as a drunk," she proudly says. One woman's husband and dad just left one day. John, Paula's youngest boy, lost one of his front teeth today. Peter, a guy who's been here over a year, is paralyzed on the right side, the result of a stroke at a young age.

Carl says I'm his woman; he's been interested ever since I walked in the door. He thinks we can oil our bodies and have a nice time together. The guy next to him says, "Oil is out, honey is in." It's flattering, in an odd sort of way, but I'm not interested.

The need for community and belonging is profound. Like all people everywhere, we're social creatures, made for one another, created to move from loneliness to connectedness. This is Carl's way of saying, "I'm interested. I like you." I returned the playfulness. It was harmless fun, and remained part of the way in which Carl and I related to each other. He and I just seemed to click. That happens too.

There's a lot of hooking up in the shelter. Living from shelter to shelter is hard and lonely; knowing that you can trust someone, a special someone, is as important in the lives of the homeless as it is for anyone. Carl's remarks were a sign of acceptance, that I was okay, desirable, part of the group. Wrapped around this sense of desirability is one of fear and caution. I have yet to learn the fine line between kidding around and testing the waters. They always run hand in hand, but interpreting the signs takes time.

It's important to be part of a community, to be part of the creation of new relationships. It is not enough just to have acquaintances; connections are critical, connections of the heart and mind. It's not pretty here. The love is often harsh, but it is sacrificial. People give themselves for each other. The same passion that causes two guys to fight releases two people to love. It was from the cross that Jesus made the new family. To John he said, "Look, here is your mother," and to Mary, "Here is your son." In the shelter, it's not about class or race, schooling or jobs; it's about staying with someone when they are dying inside.

SEEING THE NEW YEAR WITH NEW EYES

December 31

The SSI checks are coming, straight to the bank; many have spent theirs already. The young boy who just lost his tooth wants a robot.

There are no phone calls, no mail, no questions or decisions, no possessions. Just stay on time for meals and for the bus to the shelter. But I still have too much to carry. My jacket is heavy and my hat is a weight upon my head. I'm sitting on a bench in the mall; everything looks so good. A haircut is fifty dollars. Coffee is two dollars or more. I hope they'll let me sit here even though I don't buy anything.

Today, in the community room, we talked about religion. We had nonbelievers, a few born-again Christians, and lots of others, just listening. One man was a former Baptist minister who was always reading a book. He was good looking, strong and lean, with red hair. He had a wife and five children, and he drank his way out of a church and a marriage. A lot of people in the room understood what he was going through, but they didn't always understand how a preacher could go wrong. Except Bobby, because he too called himself a preacher, though no one really believed him, and he had been in the shelter for years. "I ain't gonna believe nothin' of your religion," shouted Carl, "unless you can answer one question. Now listen to me, Preacher Boy, and hear me through. How many children did Adam and Eve have?" "Three," said the preacher man, even though others thought there were only two. "Now listen to me. Cain killed Abel, right." "Right," came the response. "Now, when Cain killed Abel and God kicked him out of the garden, Cain met all them other people! Now tell me, Preacher Boy, where did all them people come from?" Now, that was a tough question and many people gave different answers. But Preacher Boy didn't fare any better than the others. Carl's eyes twinkled, a broad smile crossed his face, and with a hearty, triumphal laugh, he said, "Until you answer that question, I ain't believ'n.'"

I have such a sense of freedom. One pair of pants, boots, a jacket, and a backpack. No worries, not in charge of or responsible for anything. I play 1000 rummy most of the afternoon with Carl, Izzy, and Wayne. They tease me. Carl is interested in me, wants a smart woman to match him. I'm learning that many of the men like me. I am flattered, and happy. It is safe in the community room and shelter. Serious conversation creeps into the teasing. Some hold court; others are held by the court. I have a peaceful feeling; the rat race is over. Not much is hidden here. There is mostly raw emotion. "F—" is the most common word. Money is the main topic, food is the most wanted gift, and sex is behind every conversation.

It is New Year's Eve. I have been given a blue button to pin on my jacket that reads, "First Night 2002." The button will get me into all the New Year's Eve events sponsored by the city. Everyone at Crossoads should have been given a button, but at 5 p.m. we have to take the bus to the shelters, away, unseen by those coming into the city for the festivities. I ask why everyone wasn't given a button, and was told by other homeless people, "they don't want to see us. They don't want us around." The city officials don't want other people to feel unsafe. Who's safe? The people at First Night? The people at the shelters? None of us? We live in unsafe times. "Get behind me, fear," I say. I don't want to give in to all the anxiety. It can be paralyzing if you let it in.

As I walk the streets, I am nervous that someone will recognize me with the big lips and ugly lipstick. There's not much difference between looking like a beloved clown and a half-witch. Children look at me with big eyes, but they don't cry. I go to Grace Church's Mandolin Concert; looking around,

I scout out the audience. Who do I have to watch out for, who might recognize me? I sit in the back with another homeless person.

"Food," says the sign outside the door of another church, so I go inside, but it was all for sale; proceeds only to the homeless. "Sorry," they say, "no food for free."

I decide to hawk my First Night button. There it is, the button sales booth. A guy reaches for his wallet, and I say, "Want to buy a button?" "How much?" "Six bucks." Another guy walks up with a button. "I'll sell mine for five dollars." So the guy with a date buys both buttons for eleven dollars. It would have cost him twenty-four dollars. I was nervous, real nervous; what if the police were around? Is it illegal? I think so. But I feel good. In control. Six dollars is a good amount when I have only two hundred dollars for the month.

"The mark of a simple mind is someone who makes things complicated," says a guy on the bus.

Walking around the city on New Year's Eve as a homeless person helped me to see, once again, the great disparity of wealth in our country. Fancy restaurants were filled with people eating twenty-five dollar entrees and drinking good bottles of wine. On the street were warmly dressed couples, leaning into each other as they walked from one event to another. Some folks were ice-skating, and others were purchasing food and souvenirs from kiosk vendors. In the corners, sitting on the steps, huddled by the side of buildings, with bags by their sides and a boom box in the middle of a group, were a couple of guys with skateboards. They couldn't afford the twelve dollar entry fee for indoor events, but they celebrated the night drawing warmth from each other. What will be our New Year's resolutions? Certainly, they will all be personal. What corporate resolutions are we willing to make? It's not enough just to pray for those who are in need.

NOW IT'S PEANUT BUTTER

January 1, 2003

I am very sick, and I keep falling asleep in a chair. I am having dinner at St. Stephen's, and no one recognizes me. All the clients are very polite. We like the food. We are grateful for what we receive. Earlier this morning conversation turned to God again, Cain and Abel and "them other people in the world." Preacher Boy repeated his explanation. He's low key, good with people.

Carl says, "You're my girl, Aly. We're gonna put peanut butter on our bodies and get together."

I'm so sick, I go home. I sleep twelve hours. I didn't want to go home, but I thought it best. When I wake up, I feel better and return to Crossroads. Most of the people at Crossroads have someplace to go when they're sick. Relatives will let them in for a night or two. Still, I am aware of my privilege to return home.

I meet with my case manager. She's very nice. She wants to help me get gloves, a library card, and a job. I walk to the library, but they say I need a fax form from Crossroads since I don't have an address. I return to Crossroads, but my case manager is at lunch. Later she says that she hasn't heard about the library needing a fax, but she'll look into it.

Carl says, "I'm about to explode and nobody should bother me." He's a very large man and could knock my head off.

There are about eighty people sitting at tables and around the room at Crossroads. First we have donut holes someone donated, then sliced beef, pasta, potatoes, and spinach pie. Crossroads doesn't cook meals; it just distributes donations. The food isn't heated, so most things are cold or at room temperature.

Tonight I'm in bed by 11 p.m., and the woman in bed 2 thinks she had a miscarriage. Everyone is giving her advice: signs, symptoms, what to do next. She is very sad because she always wanted a child, and she and her man plan to marry later in the year. She says that she had an ultrasound yesterday and was going to the hospital tomorrow at noon to get the results.

At exactly 12:45 the next day, I see her coming out of a commercial building, not the hospital. She introduces me to Billy. I ask her how she is and how the hospital went. "Forget the hospital. I'll go another day; I'm fine." I figure that Billy was her trick, because earlier in the morning she said that she was going to the bank to meet her pimp and that she was going back to prostitution.

I tell her to be careful because you never know what someone might have. "Oh, I get my men through my book; they're not just off the street. They take care of me. This coat from a man, these gloves from a man. Oh, yeah, I do real well, and

I get money, too." It turns out she wasn't pregnant, didn't have a miscarriage, and didn't have any children.

Wayne has just returned from the blood plasma bank. He gives twice a week. The first day he gets twenty-five dollars and the second fifteen dollars. That's forty dollars a week.

Greg and Carl are talking near the trash can. Carl's eyes are cruising around the room, seeing who's looking or listening. It looks like they've got some deal going. I keep thinking I've seen Greg before, around town, hanging out. A man called Popeye looks familiar too. His lips are where his teeth used to be, all sunken in, and he's very thin and short.

Carl returns to his chair and is talking to a white guy, calling him "my brother." "He ain't your brother," says a woman. "You don't tell me who my brother is." "Oh, yeah?" "Well, you don't look nothing alike." "That's because we're goin' back many generations." "Well, what is the one thing you's have in common? Nothing!" "Oh, yes we do," he said, lowering his voice to a stage whisper. "A small penis." Everyone laughs.

It takes a lot to be poor:

It takes patience, because nothing comes when it is supposed to come.

It takes energy, because going to meal sites is draining. You may have to walk some distance even when it's cold outside.

It takes restraint, because anger can lead to having your head taken off. Tempers are often on edge. It doesn't take too many matches to start a fire.

It takes trust, because there is no certainty as to where your next meal is coming from, or what it will be, or when it's too far to walk to the place where they're serving a meal. At Crossroads it's usually donuts, bread, or pasta, never fruit or vegetables. Usually it's worth going to a meal site.

There are limitations when you're poor; there's just so much you can carry around.

But the poor are rich in some ways; certainly in time, humor, and community as they watch out for each other.

Maybe I'm poor, lacking time, personal freedom, independence from the expectations and projections of others, so much of which is difficult for me to identify.

A Journal of Days

Now I have freedom from:

mundane tasks	*identities*
phone calls	*worry*
mail	*personalities*
schedules	*being in charge*
calendars	*projection*
meetings	*everyone's expectations*
belongings	*stress*
cooking	*anxiety*
responsibilities	*judgment*
decisions	*negativity*
roles	

Now I have freedom to:

think	*wander*
listen	*enter different worlds*
let go	*learn*
receive	*do nothing*
be empty	*not be known*

make up a fairy tale (some would say lie)
create a new role and identity
get lost in a crowd, even in church
wear the same clothes
have no bag or purse and only one pair of shoes

be entrusted with new secrets:
  "I'm a prostitute"
  "I did eleven years for armed robbery"
  "I used to deal in drugs"
  "I'm still not completely clean"
Now I have freedom to talk, to shmooze.

SEX IS TOPIC NUMBER ONE

January 2

They constantly talk about sex in the community room. Who's doin' it, when, with whom, and how much everyone needs it, but I don't see much action. We all spend the day together in the common room, and as soon as we get to Welcome Arthur, we're separated with males and females on different floors. But the talk is endless: the shelter, sex, Jews, Palestinians, secret societies, sex again, cigarettes. The loud ones gather together around tables and keep the action going. The quieter ones sit on the side and listen and watch, or talk one-on-one.

I like being a cat: sleeping and not sleeping, watching and not watching, always listening.

A Journal of Days

January 3

They walk into Crossroads wearing royal blue jackets and dark blue pants and sporting big white block letters: POLICE. The room goes quiet, except for a woman with a squeaky voice: "How yous doin; looking for som'un?" She turns to the rest of us in the room, "Hey, y'all be good now."

The guy next to me says, "I ain't worried; I ain't done nothing. They ain't looking for me." The police stand in front of one of the guys seated at a table and ask, "How are you?" The man turns his face a quarter way round so he is looking right at the policeman. The policemen move on. These guys are big men, well fed, tall. One has a woolen mask on; just come in from the cold. They're looking at another man.

The director of Crossroads walks in, as does my caseworker. Everyone is cool. After checking out the men's room, the police leave. Wayne reaches into his pocket, smiles, and gives me a packet of hot chocolate.

Pat, my caseworker, tells me that she's faxed the necessary papers to the library and I can use their computer thirty minutes a day. She's also signed me up for job training. I told her that I'd like to do maintenance, that I've done it before, but that I don't want to buff floors.

It's begun to snow, and I go to Dunkin' Donuts to cash in some coupons I found on the street for a bagel. The main street is blocked by the rescue squad. A guy is on a stretcher, but by the time I reach the scene he has been put in the ambulance. I wonder if he is one of ours. Probably. This place can be a dead-end street. Literally.

It's so hard to get a job. You can't get a job that pays enough to live on, and the waiting list for low-income housing is at least two years. You can't get medical insurance. The food is all carbs. The shelters are filling up. You have to get to Welcome Arthur early, but they still don't open the doors until 5 p.m., so you have to wait outside in the cold.

On the radio I hear that a big celeb isn't going to be picked up for something she did. Some of these guys have been picked up for what they haven't done.

January 3, Evening

Jamie is so high tonight; manic; acting out; sexual gyrations in her boyfriend's boxer shorts. Giggling, talking loudly. Linda is her sole audience and Jamie loves it: total and complete attention from another person. "I hate my hair; it's turning green." "Who the hell wants green hair?" "Bed 2 is my bed, ain't it, Linda?" "Every time I'm here," says Jamie, "bed 2 is mine, right under the picture of 9/11. That's my picture. Got to have it over my bed."

"Last week I had bed 2." I say, "but any time you want it you can have it." "I only come about two or three times a month; know what I mean?" she asks. "Then things change, and I come back." Later at dinner, Jamie eyes a four-year-old girl who shows us her sheet of heart-shaped tattoos. "Hey," says Jamie, "these are sexy. Yea, you is gonna look real sexy." "Look at these sexual tattoos," she says as she showed them to the people at the dinner table. I looked at the four year old and say, "They're beautiful tattoos. They're hearts, and they say that you are very lovable." She smiles.

After dinner, I watch TV with the guard and another client. Together, we are real good at Wheel of Fortune. We win every game. The guard talks about Jamie; always on coke or heroin. She just got her methadone and is flying pretty high. No wonder she doesn't have custody of her four-year-old son. "Hey, isn't this the same woman who a few days ago told me she didn't have any children?"

By the time 9 p.m. comes around, everyone is quiet and the lights are turned off.

It's the homeless children who are most painful to watch. What kind of life do they have? Why should they be subjected to people like Jamie? Too many children live in poverty. It makes me sick to my stomach. Why should any child have to worry about hunger and shelter, school and clothing? What's wrong with the rest of us?

THE STREET SHEET FOR FREE MEALS

January 4, Saturday

A woman walks over to me, hunched over her walker. She suffers from severe back pains, and she can't stand up straight. She's on the list for housing, and asks me to share an apartment with her for two hundred fifty a month. "We'd both be better off," she says. It is a generous and kind invitation and it is difficult not to be encouraging, yet encouragement of such a relationship can only result in grave disappointment. The desire to help someone must have boundaries. Always.

I look at the street sheet this morning: the list of places to get breakfast, lunch, and dinner.

I go to a church in Olneyville that serves breakfast for the homeless. I have half a glass of grapefruit juice, coffee, and pancakes and don't eat the meat and potatoes. It is delicious.

Kathy shares her story with me. She has three children ages two, twenty, and twenty-one. At one time she had an apartment and a job and lived with her children. But when her third child was born it was difficult to do everything. The child agency in another state claimed she was an unfit mother. The father of her youngest child doesn't pay child support. The middle daughter now has a child, and both live with Kathy's mother. Kathy is looking for an apartment where they can live together. She also wants to find a job.

A company sometimes comes to Crossroads to hire people who are willing to hold signs all day for a furniture company. I remember seeing people holding signs by the side of the road like live advertising posts. I was told that the company people come at 10:30 a.m., give you lunch and a few cigarettes, and pay about five dollars an hour or twenty-five dollars for the day. I wait, but when they don't come I decide to go to the Convention Center. A few nights ago, a grand advertisement on TV showed a sale of brand-name items at reduced prices. It looked like a flea market, so I go. What else is there to do? Today there are too many people at Crossroads. Anyone who had someplace else to go was encouraged to leave. I thought the flea market was for free. When I got to the Convention Center they ask me for five dollars. After much hesitation, I break down and pay the fee. But the show isn't at all like the advertisement. Not more than half of the Convention Center is open. It's a sham. I don't want to go in. The ticket taker tells me that I can complain to management on the fourth floor, Room C. When I knock on the door, a woman opens it a crack, and I tell her how disappointed I am. She isn't happy, but she takes my ticket stub and gives me five dollars. No questions. No happy face. She may not like what she did, but I am grateful. It makes me think. Even when we do things out of frustration or the desire to get rid of someone, we may be doing the other person a great favor.

From the age of about ten to when I was four-teen, I used to be mesmerized by the *New York*

Times "Neediest Cases," published for a few weeks around Christmas. I'd read them by the hour; synopses of tragic family situations for which money was needed. I experienced a strange affinity, and I learned strong lessons about the complexities of life. At times, I was reduced to tears, seeing myself as a youngster in one of the case studies. It was a heartbreaking lesson in tragedy not discussed at home or in the classroom. It awakened feelings of my own fragility and how easy it is to break. I also felt a sense of helplessness. The children could do nothing, and their parents had already gotten them in trouble. The next Sunday I would read them again, a new set of case stories. But after Christmas, I'd have to wait another year before they appeared again, because the campaign was over. I realize now that I'd always experienced an authenticity and integrity about the "neediest." The sad stories touched all my needs for security, peace, boundaries, and consistency. They also touched some inner fear that terrible things would happen to me.

I'm writing all of this in the lobby of the Westin Hotel, and no one has asked me what I'm doing here or told me to leave.

He beckons me from an alley. He introduces himself as Robert. "I'm Aly," I say. "You work down there?" he asks, motioning to Crossroads. "Me? No I don't work there. I stay there during the day." "You work there?" I ask. "No, I don't work there." "Come here," he says, motioning to the alley. "No, you come here," I say from the street. "Okay, okay. You got a man?" "Kind of." "Okay, I was gonna ask ya for money, you know, a dollar or two." "Yea, if I had a dollar or two, I wouldn't be goin' to Crossroads for some food." "How about coming with me to my mother's house?" "No, thanks; I gotta get to Crossroads in time for lunch." "I don't mean to cause you no trouble. Just want to talk awhile at my mother's house. I ain't putting you on." "No, you're not putting me on; you're a good man, I just have to go to Crossroads. I'm hungry." "I'll take you to my mother's for lunch sometime. See y'around." "Yeah," I say, "see you around sometime."

I go to the Church of the Epiphany soup kitchen at 4 p.m. and have a great meal: chicken, rice, salads, dessert. It's served by kids from St. Luke's youth group: Emily, Andrew, Andrew, Alex, and others. Ken, the youth leader, was there, too. It's the best meal I've had since being on the streets.

I was very honored to be served by the young people from one of my parishes, and to watch how generously they acted toward the homeless.

January 5, Sunday

I slept very well last night. Bed 5 is just right. Kathy did my laundry in exchange for $1.25 in quarters. It's always good to carry around quarters. My wash consists of one long underwear shirt, one long underwear bottom, one pair of white socks, one pair of brown socks, and one pair of underpants. Turning clothes inside out gives them a few more days of wear.

I'm sitting in St. Mary's Church, waiting for the 8 a.m. Eucharist. Bright rays of sun are catching the brilliant colors and shapes of newly restored stained glass windows, reflecting an array of color and light on everything east. Here is the brightness of Jerusalem calling us to all the beauty framed in the rays of peace. Glass next to glass, bonded by lead, colors in their own frames finding identity in relationship with other pieces of glass and the unpredictability that light brings to everything in life.

The deacon is speaking to the usher. Except for me, only one other person is here. Later, during the announcements, the priest says that the parish is making sandwiches for Crossroads, and they will be adding another week sometime during the year. They give one week a year now. Downstairs I find boxes of beautifully fresh oranges, and when I ask if I can have one, the woman in the kitchen is very nice and says, "Please take one." The priest is kind, humorous, not at all the same as when I've seen him in the company of other clergy or at meetings. Maybe he's best on his own turf.

It's Sunday and there is nothing to do. A couple of hours later I go to the Church of St. Peter and St. Paul. I look ridiculous; a safety against suffering the mortification of being recognized. But no one pays any attention to me. Either they are used to seeing street people, or they don't know how to respond or what to say. I have a sudden urge to be Jesus. Standing at the front door, I welcome people in my lisping Aly voice. "Hello, sister in Jesus. Hello, brother in Jesus," I say. A few nod, some say hello, but only two people really look at me. A three, or four-year-old smiles and waves, but her parents sweep her away before I can say anything else. I go into the church, and to each person who comes my way, I say again, "Hello, my sister in Jesus. Hello my brother in Jesus." One person smiles at me. Even the leaflet distributors, ushers, and greeters keep their distance.

Church is good. After the service I am told that there is food downstairs; just a few cakes. So once again, I stand near the door downstairs, "Hello, my sister in Christ." Then all of a sudden one person responds, "Have we met before?" The truth is we saw each other at the mall the day before, and we exchanged only a brief glance. But she remembers and shakes my hand and introduces herself and wants to know my name. Her name is Alexi Warren.

Back at Crossroads, the fire rescue squad comes to take away a woman who had been in tears a half-hour earlier. I am leaving to go to the library when a member of the rescue squad says, "Hello, Bishop Wolf." "Oh, you must be thinking of my cousin; she's in Honduras," I say congenially and walk on, feeling panicky inside. The fireman follows me down the street, certain of who I am. I have to blow my cover with him, but he is terrific, understanding, and helpful. He says he can make arrangements for me to ride in the rescue car sometime. I calm down and realize it is okay to be recognized by some people, as long as it doesn't happen very often. I am pleased that I handled it well and so did the fireman. I am afraid that if my cover is blown, my relationship with the homeless will end.

I wait at the bus stop for half an hour. A tired looking woman in her thirties, with three young boys reflecting their mother's weariness in their own faces and demeanor, come to the stop. Three young boys with their worn-down mother. They had an apartment for quite a while and one day they received a notice in the mail telling them that the building had been sold and they would have to vacate their apartment in thirty days. Since it took nine days for the letter to reach them, they had twenty-one days left. The mother knew the building wouldn't change hands right away so she volunteered to continue paying rent and to paint the apartment if they could stay. It didn't work out, so she and the boys are living at the shelter. She thinks they'll be placed in an apartment soon, but only for a month. "Why only a month?" I ask. "That's the way they do things."

Having heard many other similar experiences, I question "the way they do things," and I burn inwardly with frustration. Then I find out that she is a loud, destructive person. She was asked to leave all the shelters; only Welcome Arthur would take her.

Bear one another's burdens, and in this way you will fulfill the law of Christ. Galatians 6:2

We must all carry the burden of the homeless, lost, handicapped, and addicted. It is the burden of society. It is the burden we bear as members of God's creation. If we didn't carry each other's burdens, we'd all fall beneath the weight of them.

Shelly, the matron, has just told us that Leah is being switched into room 303. Leah usually stays by herself in a very small room, but the men's rooms are full, so a few men will use Leah's room. Many women from room 303 start to complain, citing health reasons. Leah has "problems," and since she has been assigned to the bed next to mine, I ask what the problems are. Maybe she snores loudly or talks in her sleep. "We ain't gonna tell you," one woman says. "Just wait," another teases me, "ya gonna find out yisself."

Later, after Dateline is over, the TV show that got the most votes from everyone in the room, I went to my bed, number 5. About half-way across the room, it hits me. It isn't urine or body odor, it isn't pungent or arresting, but there is a deep disgusting smell that infiltrates every air particle and must have already passed into my lungs. I can feel it filling every interior space of my body. I open the window and try to catch my breath. When I return to my bed, the smell has dissipated somewhat. Leah has placed a blanket over her whole body. "It ain't that she doesn't take a shower," from a woman across from me, "but what's wrong with her is that she is sick and she needs a doctor. A friend of mine smells just like that. They had to cut her open. They found maggots. You's never know what's goin on, but she's sick. They ain't supposed to have anyone in here who's a health hazard."

It was disgusting, but she didn't smell as bad as some; at least it wasn't stale urine or feces. Alleviated by the cold air from the window and the blanket covering her, my nose accommodated to the remaining odor. My ear plugs hushed her deep and labored breathing.

WHO IS MY NEIGHBOR?

January 6

A new mayor, Cicillini, is being sworn in today. Some guys are joking because he's gay. I suggest we all go to the city hall steps and show our support. Carl says we need rent control. Something's got to give with the lack of affordable housing. "They're turning this into a tourist state and forgetting about the people who live here," Carl says. There are about a thousand people who brave the light snow and watch David Cicillini's swearing in.

There is a special room at Crossroads for children and families, but it has very few toys and nothing creative like paper, paint, pens, Legos; just coloring books; everything to be drawn within the lines. The mothers color and the children color, but it is not enough. The only thing the coloring books do is stifle imaginations and encourage boredom, fighting, and tears. No one donates good, safe craft items and toys to a homeless shelter.

Someone in the regular adult room found some plastic bits on the street. Souvenirs from the New Year's Eve weekend, they are broken pieces of stars, wands, and lights. I give them to Kerrie, who is about six. It takes no time for her to re-create the pieces and make something to play with.

I would like to bring some of my unpainted wood and paint to the room, but it's not allowed because I'm not related to the children. Of course, it makes sense considering potential abuse and insurance issues. The director, Anne Nolan, told me that I could contribute after I return to my normal life's pattern as a bishop.

Bernadette stays with her children, Kelly, six, and Megan, two. She wants to go to school for some vocational training, but she doesn't qualify for day care. Her husband, their father, has a full-time job in the southern part of the state. He lives in a different shelter so that he is closer to his job. They've been homeless for almost a year. After interviewing for many places, they were turned down because they have children and can only afford a small apartment. They are on a waiting list for subsidized housing.

People are in shelters for many reasons:

- emotional illness: there is no home for them or not enough psychiatric care, or they have trouble taking their medicines

- physical disability: they can't climb steps, or they're in a wheelchair, and no one has an accessible apartment for them

- chronic alcoholism or drug addiction

- working poor: they can't live in Rhode Island on eight dollars an hour. They say that a living wage is closer to eleven dollars, but who pays that much?

- age limitations

- a criminal record

- SSI: they make six hundred dollars a month from the government. The average studio apartment is almost five hundred, plus security and a deposit. They might as well spend their money on decent food and a bus ticket.

That evening, a slim gray-haired woman of about seventy, wearing a flower-print dress over blue slacks and sneakers, walks into the communal bedroom carrying a clean towel in her hand. In a high-pitched voice she says, "I didn't want to discuss anything, but I've had enough with Will and now with the two of you." She goes over to her bed and carefully puts on the one sheet she had been given. Pulling the old blanket over her head, she giggles like a schoolgirl, as if entering a wonderful and secret place of pure joy.

One of the other women in the room calls out to her, "How about telling us about it so we can all laugh?" But the woman just keeps giggling to herself. It is infectious and tragic.

Sometimes the same woman talks coherently on a number of subjects, but the succeeding discussions never seem to connect with the previous ones. She makes random comments, including some about Will's need for a sex change. At times, I feel as if I'm watching an exquisite performance by a theatrical actress, but she is not acting. She lives with her fears and the belief that she is the government's most wanted person. Her paranoia led her to this state. "I wrote to the government and told them that I was in great distress. They didn't help me, but at least I wrote them."

"Sex without your consent is against the law. It creates violent emotions, sex you don't like. I don't like it. They like it," she says. The demons dwell inside her head. She is being tortured in our presence.

The woman in bed 4 has a high-pitched snore. Its powerful rhythm is driving me crazy. If only she would miss a beat. I'm not even sure a sleeping pill, earplugs, and a radio will muffle the sound. I keep my radio close to my ear all night. I can't find my earplugs. I wish I had a sleeping pill.

Earlier that evening I washed my clothes. When I took them out of the washer, there was fuzz on everything; my jacket had ripped in the wash, my beautiful jacket from the Salvation Army. My only jacket. The down had gotten on everything.

THINKING ABOUT MY PAST

January 7

I'm thinking of my own past, my personal home-lessness, all the moves we made when I was young, all the different schools. Bedford Elementary was my favorite, and Mr. Judell, he was so much fun.

Someone left a door open, and that horrible beeping won't stop and it's driving me crazy.

Down and Out in Providence

Yes, Mr. Judell, my favorite teacher. But at the end of the fourth grade, on the last day of school, I found out that though Mr. Judell was teaching fifth grade next year, I would not be in his class. He had the smarter students. At the time it was a terrible rejection; it felt as if it would ruin my whole year and my whole future. At ten years old my grandfather and Mr. Judell were the only men that I knew who were really fun.

Over the summer, my parents decided to move again; I wouldn't have been in Mr. Judell's class anyway. We went from a small town in Connecticut to a high-rise apartment building in Queens, but that was short-lived. We went to Douglaston, New York, and then to Cherry Hill, New Jersey, all within two years. Always on the move. Never much time to say goodbye and increasingly difficult to say hello. Always adapting to a given situation, always entering a pre-existing set of expectations, ever part of the process.

For some reason, last night I felt the horror of rejections, the emptiness created by moving. Everything seemed to be getting out of control. The TV was too loud, the guard didn't turn the light off at nine, the woman next to me had to take a late shower because she missed one earlier, and then she snored with her total body heaving up and down.

I know why people always want the same bed at the shelter, the same table in the community room. How else can anyone create a place of their own and a sense of stability? If you always have the same bed, you know where the bathroom is and how to get there. When you have a sense of place, you can have a sense of family.

Preacher Boy, the Baptist minister, spent the night in the hospital. He didn't know that his few drinks, coupled with his heart medicine, would create such adverse effects. Wayne spent the night with him, and they both returned to Crossroads after three in the morning. Crossroads is crowded again today, no chairs, lots of loud voices.

I went to see Anne Nolan, and I told her that I think it's time for me to go to another shelter. So here I am at the Family Shelter in Warwick. It was supposed to be closed down because St. Francis Church could have sold it for $500,000. It was a difficult situation. The church owns the property, and the parish needs money for its ongoing operations and ministry. Between the Roman Catholic Diocese of Providence and various donations, $500,000 was found to support the church and keep the shelter open.

It was cold out today, below freezing.

My head hurts from when I smacked it on Anne's car door last Friday. It is very sore, making the cries of babies in this family shelter even more difficult to bear. The intake is very long.

> For an hour, sitting
> Sitting for an hour
> It is now four o'clock
> Time for sitting
> > An hour for sitting
> > With my head splitting
> > Sitting just to sit
> Thinking of my head
> "Don't touch it"
> "We'll be with you in a minute"
> Just relax and sit
> For a minute
> For a minute
> For a minute

For a minute
"We're not ready for you yet"
It's that time of day
Always much to do
Relax and sit
"Read the rules and regulations"
Know our "family" expectations
I'll be back to check you in
It's real busy around here
A few minutes, a few minutes

You'll be in a room
        Small, for one
It's not ready
        Someone lives there
She'll be moving to a
        Room for two
You'll be in her room
        When the move is through
Leave your things over there
        Under lock and key
They'll be safe for now
You can watch TV
Soon it will be dinner

Ah, it's finally ready
       Tasty meat, salad, even spaghetti
"Where is the ladies' room?"
          I patiently inquire
But another hour passes and
          Inside begins a fire
And I try to hold frustration
          Without too much success
"Excuse me but I'm tired and I
          Need a good night's rest
Tell me where there is a toilet
And how about my room"
She could sense my aggravation
Her response was extra smooth
       "Please let me help you, it's
          Such a busy time
       But that's no excuse the fault
          Was mine"
       She's a nice woman, sure and
          Clear
Professional, honest
          Relief was near.
This is not a good place to be
          Cause I'm not a part of
          The scenery

A Journal of Days

No children, no focus, no shared
Anxiety and age
Tomorrow it's Crossroads
This isn't my page

A beautiful, tall black woman was laid off from her job at a large bank. (I thought, I'm not surprised; I think that was the bank that invested heavily in Argentina and has lost a lot of money.) She couldn't pay her rent; hers was a low-paying job. Thankfully, she found a new job in a month, but her landlord had already sent her on her way. She and her daughter wound up in the shelter, and now she's looking for an apartment. She has filled out endless forms and has only so many hours in a day to work, look for an apartment, and be with her eleven-year-old daughter.

Another woman is waiting for her four-year-old to be returned to her in two days. The Department of Children, Youth, and Families took the daughter away when the mother and father became homeless. Her husband is legally blind and on SSI. She cares for their three children, two of whom are living with relatives. But there wasn't enough room in the home for the four-year-old, so she was put into a foster home. Now, since the mother is in a family shelter and has been approved for Section 8 housing, the four-year-old will live with her in the shelter.

In the meantime, the mother spends every day filling out forms and hunting for an apartment. She found the perfect one for four hundred dollars a month, a sum the family can afford. But the landlord won't rent to anyone who earns less then seventeen hundred dollars a month.

I take a shower and wash the dye out of my hair. My scalp itched so much and the dye was so thick that I washed it out in spite of the cold water. It was so awful it took four washings to wash it out. I thought I would scratch my head through to my skull. Even after four washings it could use another.

Having a room of one's own in this shelter is nice, but the talking in the hallway on the other side of the door is no gift. Nothing can deaden the whines and cries of the babies.

There's a small window in the room, and I can just see the moon nestled in the night sky, like a hammock, inviting me to rest in its beauty.

A SACRED RESPONSIBILITY TO HONOR THE PEOPLE

January 8

> Typical, blame blame
> Name game
> No one wants things to stay the same
> Eight voices speaking
> Most squeaking
> Wanting more than they are getting
> Not enough stuff,
> A real frustration
> Government funds are like a ration
> Just enough to plant a seed,
> not enough to meet the need
> Everyone trying
> Pulling together
> Staff and clients to make things better
> The hot voices are cooling
> Good ideas take form
> We're all trying hard to get along

Typical blame game. It's always someone else's fault, but the power of the group is revealed once again. There are people who name the truth, recognizing how easy it is to blame others, and they even have some good suggestions that could be implemented immediately: clean your table.

I'm still painfully aware about how differently I am treated as a homeless person. When I am in a store, people are suspicious. When I'm in the street, people turn their eyes to the sidewalk.

My glasses are all twisted; I can't see anything. The other night I put them in my boots, and when I awoke, I stepped into my boots, forgetting that the eyeglasses were in one of them.

I have to get my glasses fixed. The first eyeglass store says that they only fix glasses sold by their store. The second place says they only do Lasik surgery and don't even have tools to fix glasses. The third place is just right. An older man dressed in a white shirt and tie asks where I purchased the glasses. Not that it matters. He then proceeds to fix the arms and straighten out the frame. They fit just right.

I apply for a job at a large hotel this morning. Where the application reads "address," I write in the address of Crossroads. Where it requests telephone number, I leave it blank. How can I get a job without an address and phone number? I fill out the application still thinking of the people in the Family Shelter. Many of them work. The problem is the rents; they're too high. Maybe we should change our diocesan low-income housing units from elderly to family. I'm just wondering how I can make a difference. How can I drop a small stone into a huge ocean? I feel helpless. There is so much to be done. Where can I start? How?

⌒

Anne Nolan wants the story of Crossroad to be told. In fact, part of the deal for her help in this venture was that I would let a reporter follow me occasionally. She arranged for me to meet the reporter from the *Providence Journal.* We are sitting in Anne's office. I hope the woman doesn't continue to ask more questions. She wants to come to church with me, and I'm not sure about it. Church is a spiritual time for me. I don't want to be followed by a reporter.

The director of the Family Shelter telephoned Anne, thinking that I had been a plant from the Crossroads board. So I'm sitting on Anne's car as she and Michelle, the assistant director of Cross-roads, work things out with the staff at the shelter. Michelle has grave misgivings about what I am doing and the deceit that it involves. Of course she is right. The deception goes against the agency's values. Deception goes against my values too, but I know that the decision to remain anonymous was right.

All of this brings to mind the extraordinary people who devote their lives to helping others. First, the director of the Family Shelter, whose intuition was so keen that she recognized her misgivings regarding me and immediately telephoned Anne, her supervisor.

Michelle is so honest, full of integrity, and communicative, with no emotions held back, testing me with her questions. Like a good mother she shelters her clients: the homeless to whom she has devoted her life. She reminds me of the fraudulency involved in this, for I have a home and I have choices and I am not homeless. She gently smacked me with truth and reminded me of my sacred responsibility to honor the people with whom I share the day and to use my position to help the homeless to reposition their lives.

A Journal of Days

I am beginning to get anxious about this sacred trust of human lives that has been given to me. It is increasingly difficult to justify my actions. I am struck by the pure honesty and dedication of both staff and clients. The clients are people who only ask for a chance, their faces worn from looking for bare necessities, for themselves and their children. And the children reach out to those who will hold and love them.

Tonight is loud and anxious at the shelter. Jamie is either high or has had more than the beer she confessed to drinking. It is the first time that I have been afraid. "I hate that bitch," snarls Jamie, referring to another homeless woman, "I'd like to beat her up to a pulp, but she's a cop caller. I ain't touchin' her, but I'm gonna bug that bitch so that she hits me and then I'm gonna make it so she doesn't walk anymore. No. I ain't getting in trouble because of her. I can get someone else to take care of her."

The reporter from the *Providence Journal* visits Crossroads, and she is introduced as someone who is doing a story about the homeless. She's visiting Welcome Arthur tonight!

When the reporter, Jennifer, comes to room 303, everyone has something to say: the conditions, lack of jobs, lack of cleanliness, difficulty in finding apartments. There is excitement and hopefulness; energy is released because someone important is listening. A woman from another room comes in. "Don't forget about us in the room over there. We're waitin' for ya. A lotta people have a lot to say."

January 9

"Hamburger" touches too much when he talks to me. He's already professed his interest, but today when he touches my thigh I say, "Excuse me, but I own my leg."

"I get my apartment in two weeks, and I'm getting all new furniture," he says. "Where are you getting your furniture?" I ask. "My older son, he knows where to get furniture."

I take a bus into Boston and walk around with my backpack. I am so very tired. Where can I go to rest? Where can I sit? It is too cold outside. I need warmer gloves. The Paulist Center is helpful. They direct me to the St. Francis Center, but it is too far to walk, and I am already out of breath.

On the way to the Episcopal Cathedral, I see a man with a cup for contributions with a sign: "homeless because of fire." I ask him about the fire, and he tells me that the shelters are no good. They are too dangerous. He sleeps on the corner of Tremont and Park, right next to the church. And he makes sure he's across from the train so when people walk up or down the steps they will see him.

"They don't believe there are homeless people here," he tells me. "I'm articulate, moderately intelligent, and even at fifteen dollars an hour I couldn't afford an apartment in Boston." Pointing to the subway entrance, he lowers his pitch, raises his volume, and with passionate conviction says, "I don't want them to forget."

"Now, I measure my sense of worth by the simple fact that someone looks me in the eye," he says, "and when I ask a question, if they actually take the time to help me."

There he is, sitting in front of one church, down the street from another church, diagonally across from a cathedral, and a few steps from one of the oldest churches in Boston. Church people are generous to those in need, but how much can a church respond with limited resources?

Some of the churches are warm and welcoming, and others are locked up. I walk into one church, and no one even looks at me, no one welcomes me.

So instead of loving what you think is peace,
  love others, and love God above all.
And, instead of hating the people
  you think are warmongers,
  hate the appetite and the disorder
  in your own soul, which are the causes
    of war.
If you love peace, then hate injustice, hate
    tyranny, hate greed —
But hate those things in yourself first, not in
    another.
  — Thomas Merton, in the *Catholic Worker*

AMBASSADORS OF GOD

I learn about tips for waiters. I find out that waiters make less than three dollars an hour in most places. They rely on tips. "They also serve who only stand and wait." Where they work determines whether they'll earn enough in tips to afford an apartment. Tips in an average restaurant probably don't cut it.

Peter Maurin, in an essay published in the *Catholic Worker*, referred to people who are in need as "Ambassadors of God who give those who are not in need the opportunity to give to those who are." I suppose it's the angels unaware. I like thinking that every person in need is an ambassador of God and that I am at my ambassadorship best when I am in need.

I hope that the poor will have the courage to be present in the places of those who are comfortable. We are not generous by nature but by the birth of compassion. Compassion is not born in comfort but by being faced with one's own poverty, aloneness, and inadequacies. It is not the bright, shining face that reveals stature, but the faces of those who give voice to our hidden truths.

Hospitality is the giving and receiving from another person. Peter Maurin asks, "What if everyone had a spare room given over to a person in need, and if every parish worked with one person, one family? I ask. What if I did this?"

> People who are in need
> And are not afraid to beg
> Give to people not in need
> The occasion to do good
> For goodness' sake.
> Modern society calls the beggar
> Bum and panhandler
> And gives him the bum's rush.

> But the Greeks used to say
> That people in need
> Are ambassadors of the gods.
> Although you may be called
> Bums and panhandlers
> You are in fact the ambassadors of God.
> As God's ambassadors
> You should be given food,
> Clothing and shelter
> By those who are able to give it.
> — Peter Maurin, 1933

January 9. Evening

The chapel lights are on, and I think maybe evening prayer is being said. But when I open the chapel door, I am stunned to see an older woman at a prayer desk at the east end of the chapel facing the west door through which I had entered. In front of her are about a dozen students, barely breathing as she recites poetry from Hildegard of Bingen. At least I think it's Hildegard of Bingen.

I am frozen to the spot, believing that I have entered into her world as much as she into mine. I don't move lest I break that invisible line that connects us East to West and West to East. She is magnificent. The poetry is hers, worn into her heart by whatever she shares with the twelfth century saint, whose words and music were almost unheard of as recently as twenty-five years ago.

The words find their ending point, her voice is still, and in silence her hands close the book placed before her. Then she lifts up her arms and invites the group to join her in song and dance, and she looks at me and asks, "Would you like to join us?" I want to and I do. With my pack on my back, I join my gloved hands to those reaching out to draw me into the circle, and we give homage to God in words of love and joy at the end of the day, at the threshold between light and mystery. When the song ends, I say, "Thank you. You have been as Jesus to me," and I leave. We are all smiling together. So, Episcopal Divinity School, my seminary, the place of so much confusion and disappointment for me during the 1970s, on the close of this day becomes a place of blessing.

I am thinking about being Jesus to others as I venture on my path looking for Jesus in the poor. There are moments when I am aware of the mutuality of blessing. It is a frightful thing to think that Jesus desires to be released into the world through me. It is easier to believe that I should seek him elsewhere.

EMOTIONAL SOUP IS ALWAYS ON THE BURNER

My father is ill, and even though he does not know what I am doing this month, he expects me to visit him near Philadelphia sometime. The cheapest way to travel is by way of the Chinatown buses. From the chapel, in Cambridge, I make my way to Chinatown, in Boston, where I take the 10 p.m. bus to New York with Jennifer the newspaper reporter. Arriving at 2 a.m. on Friday, January 17, we find out that the shelter I was told to stay in doesn't exist. We go to the Fifth Precinct police station, and Officer Crowley, or maybe it's Crawley, goes to some effort to give us the names and addresses of two shelters and calls ahead to make sure there is room, an incredible act of generosity. He is helpful and respectful. We stay at the Open Door Shelter on Forty-first Street.

The matron checks our IDs and directs us to a table and brings over two chairs. There are no beds, just tables and chairs, plus lockers for those who stay on a more long-term basis. The room is relatively clean and accessible. There must be around 150 men and women sleeping on tables in two rooms. It is amazingly quiet, no snoring or coughing or talking. I think it is almost 3 a.m.

January 10

We are awakened at around 6 a.m. The woman who was sleeping immediately behind me strikes up a conversation. "I'm not goin' to tell ya anything about me, so don't ask. Nothing. I'm not goin to tell you nothin'." "You don't have to tell me anything," I say calmly." I'm going to the bathroom." I reach into my pocket, remove a tea bag, and give it to her and leave. When I return she tells me how her two-month-old baby was taken from her because she was living in the shelter. She is hoping to get a job and even an apartment sometime. She reaches into her bag and gives me a beautifully colored navel orange, a rare and special treat in the shelter. She gives one to Jennifer too.

We leave the shelter and are told that we can have breakfast at the Church of St. Francis of Assisi. The church is close to the Amtrak train station, and I have prayed there on many occasions while waiting for the train to Philadelphia or Providence. I am surprised at how disoriented and lost I am. By the time we get there, breakfast is over. Jennifer takes the train back to Providence, and I hang out around Canal Street.

It's exhausting to be homeless. Finding places to eat and sleep takes a lot of time. Being among people who have no other place to go is heartbreaking. Putting one's head on a table for months on end is like being warehoused. Even pets have decent kennels, plus wool coats and ridiculous looking booties. How can we treat our children worse than our dogs? When politicians talk about "moral values," what do they mean? I do not hear them speak of justice for our children. Certainly, moral values must not be limited to sexual attractions.

Phoebe Griswold, the wife of the presiding bishop of the Episcopal Church, meets me in front of a paint store at noon and takes me to lunch; a welcome treat. She warns me that just as Anne Nolan of Crossroads and I will have to prepare the staff and clients there for the revelation of my true identity, so I will also have to prepare the diocese. There will be some people who will be very angry about what

A Journal of Days

I experienced at some of the churches: not being welcomed, having ushers watch me, being made to feel lesser or invisible. Some of the experiences have been very sad and painful. Yet I know that I am also at fault. I haven't made the effort to reach out when visiting churches. As a parish priest I didn't welcome everyone the same way. But, sometimes, I acted beyond what I thought possible.

I'm thinking of the fellow who came to St. Mary's when I was the vicar. He was dressed shabbily, walked with a cane, and hung around the church after most of the worshipers left. I remember wanting to go home when he asked if he could see me in my office. Even though I didn't want to stay any longer, I invited him in.

He talked for a long time, about many things. Most were surprisingly interesting. Nonetheless, the clock was ticking away, and I wanted to do other things that afternoon. As he stood to leave, he reached into his pocket and took out folded bills. As he handed them to me he said, "I've been going to many churches just wanting to talk to the priest and offer a gift. Thank you," and he walked out. I counted the money: seven crisp, new hundred-dollar bills.

Phoebe and I have lunch at a cheap Chinese restaurant. She shares her respect for me and for my ministry. I feel driven, maybe compelled, I hope by the Holy Spirit of God, to keep pressing on. Life doesn't hold positive economic possibilities for many people, and I am reaping the benefits of a good life at the expense of others. I realize that I am the beneficiary of a system that allows some people to live with security while others live a marginal existence. My new acquaintances invited me into their lives without knowing my family background, the schools and colleges I attended, the jobs I've held, or the people I know. It was me, just me.

After lunch, I return to the Chinatown bus stop.

January 10, Late afternoon

I buy a bus ticket to Philadelphia Chinatown and plan to stay at the Travelers Aid there. It costs fifteen dollars because I'm going in the middle of the day. It's cheaper at night.

"Hey," a guy calls out at the bus station, "weren't you at the shelter last night?" "Yeah," I answer, "were you there?" "Yeah, I seen you there." "Do you know where there's a shelter or Travelers Aid in Philadelphia?" I ask him. "Look by the bus station," he says and then leaves with another guy. I see them standing at the top of the escalator, looking down, looking for someone or something. I wonder about him, who he and his friend are waiting for, why he lives in the shelter. But like so many others, the story is not to be told in these chance encounters.

The bus got off the turnpike at exit 4, "Moorestown Cherry Hill." I had no idea that we would be taking this route to Philadelphia. Route 73 goes from the exit to the Ben Franklin Bridge, a few miles and a thousand memories ago. First I see the mall. Then we pass the road to my high school, then I see the Pub, the hangout where Mom and Len used to have their drinks and dinner and fun. It was their club. Then we pass the Stop and Go liquor store, where Len would buy his "life blood." I didn't see the Oasis; maybe it's too dark. It's like an apartment building, and on one floor there was a recording studio they used to go to, following some singer they thought would make the big time. They would become the top fans of a famous singer. I knew these things through the ears and lenses of a fifteen-year-old, who secretly listened to the girlish giggles of a mother and future step-father in

the early, dangerous, and giddy light of their relationship. A sight, a sound, a smell, and forty years
compress into a singular moment. And, like the bus,
I just keep rolling along.

The woman at the information center at the bus
terminal in Philadelphia tells me that there is a
shelter at Broad and Arch. There isn't one. She said
it was near the Wawa food mart but the Wawa has
closed. The policeman tells me that there aren't any
local shelters, and he sends me to the police station at Ninth and Vine. I return to the bus station,
and a policewoman says that there is a shelter at
Thirteenth and Juniper. When I arrive at 7 p.m., I
am told it closed three hours earlier. Finally, I find
Eliza Shirley, a house for women, and though they
are full they let me in to wait for an open bed.

*On the third day there was a wedding in Cana of
Galilee, and the mother of Jesus was there.* John 2:1

Jesus changes water to wine. How I wish that
I could turn the water of tears into a rich wine.
The tears of little John, so tired, with his mother so
rough. They moved out of their apartment today,
two months behind in rent. She's on welfare and

sucks her thumb as she watches TV. Leelee, her five-year-old daughter is beautiful. She has light brown hair in short braids and perfect small baby teeth. Her long limbs are thin and in constant motion. She places a scarlet coat over her head and says that it is a tent. So we play tent for the next ten minutes or so. Then she starts singing a beautiful song, and she teaches it to me. We sing it together. "You two are going to drive me crazy," shouts a woman from the other side of the room. "I'm gonna hear that song in my head all night."

The song Leelee sang and taught me is one she learned in Sunday school:

> I pray for me
> I pray for you
> I need you to survive

We sang it over and over again. "I don't go to church," says her mother, "but I send her."

Kathleen worked for an elderly man for six years, caring for him in his home. She tells me a story. "One day his sister come, the one who all of a sudden is so worried about him and puts him in the hospital. Then they give him all these pills for his head, and I tell them he don't need no pills, but they say he's acting nasty, and I say, 'If he were acting nice he'd need the pills, cause his way is to be nasty.' "

I wait in the community room. All of a sudden a gaggle of kids takes over the room; every inch of it! One woman has eight children, one has two, and another also has two. Janet sits down next to me and starts working on a crossword puzzle. She's a freshman in high school and has her sights on Spellman College or NYU. She's the third of ten children and is incredibly bright and articulate.

All these kids are very well behaved. They play together while the adults read magazines. A few kids are coloring. I'm so tired. I hardly got any sleep last night. These families have rooms, but they stay in the community room and plan to watch basketball. One of the women tells me that sometimes if there aren't enough beds, you have to sleep in the community room.

Three hours later: I am assigned to room 311A. It is 10 p.m. The showers are hot, the beds are firm, and the people are wonderful; fun and humorous, but always there is a level of sadness. "Life sucks," says Sandy. She and her husband have lived in their car since June, after she lost her job. He's disabled with a bad back. They had a way of placing their belongings on the car seats so he could lie flat across the passenger side and she could sleep in the driver's seat. With no telephone and only a post office box address, she couldn't get another job. Last week someone tossed champagne bottles through their back window, and the police finally found the car. This is their first night in a shelter. She is here, and her husband is in a different one.

I don't have any clean clothes, so I turn everything inside out and wear a pair of dirty socks from a few days a ago. I wash my hair four times. That's what it takes to feel clean. It was worth using what remained in my small bottle of shampoo.

Suddenly, at 10:50 p.m., a voice on the intercom reminds all of us that we are to mop the floor and clean the bathrooms and showers. I slowly rise from the soft chair to do my share when one of the women says, "Baby, you just come here, and I can tell how tired you is. All the first time people, you jus' rest." Motioning to the others, she says, "Come on you all, let's get this done." They all go to work, made easier by the fact that the movie everyone was watching has just ended.

I am bone tired when I get onto my bed around 11:30 p.m. The lights are on, the TV is blaring, people are talking, and I still sleep soundly for seven hours.

Room 311 is a space about ten feet by ten feet divided into three areas, A, B, and C. Each area has a bed and small dresser. Sheets are distributed on the second floor, and you have to sign a form to get a sheet. A blanket is on each bed, and sometimes a pillow.

Washing clothes seems to be a problem everywhere. There are so few washers and dryers that, depending on the place, you may only get to wash once a week. Just about everyone carries most of their belongings, so there aren't that many clothes to change into.

Wilma has a job as a helper in a boarding-house. She cleans, helps patients, and does odd jobs for close to the minimum wage. She leaves the shelter by 7 a.m. and returns at 5:30 p.m., six days a week. In two weeks she'll be moving into a very small apartment. She closes her eyes and smiles.

Wherever I go, I am struck by the generosity of those who have so little. They understand about carrying heavy burdens, physical and emotional, and they always seem to have an extra pair of hands to help. An interesting emotional soup is always on the burner: humility, anger, generosity, fear, aggression, compassion. It is all here.

At around 10 a.m. I left the shelter and took a train to visit my father and his wife. They knew that I was coming but had no idea that I was living as a homeless person. I was still in the clothes that I had worn from the beginning, with my hair bushy and long. I hadn't visited my father in a few months, and when they opened the door, they were speechless. I quickly told them what I was doing. My father just shook his head. While he and Elaine didn't fully understand, they were very supportive. Dad wasn't doing too well, which made the trip to see him even more important. I returned to the shelter by midafternoon.

SHARING A MEAL

January 11

Last night I was given a tuna fish sandwich as a sign of hospitality. I wasn't very hungry, so I cut it in half. I asked whether anyone would like the other half. A very thin girl, about seven years old, came over with her bag of sour cream and onion potato chips. She shyly took the sandwich. "You want some of my potato chips?" she asked me. "Thank you," I said, and took some of the chips. I opened the sandwich and placed the chips on top of the tuna fish and replaced the slice of bread. We both looked up at the same time and took a big bite out of the sandwich. Crunch! Crunch! In one of those delightfully unplanned moments, we discovered that we at our sandwiches the same way. With mouths full we smiled tuna grins. She didn't know that anyone else put potato chips in their sandwich, nor did I.

At the next table, two women got into an argument. The exchange was getting loud and intense. Someone else said, "Keep it in. Keep it in. No reason to make a fuss over things that ain't important. Don't say no names, girls, jus' keep it in. I hear yous, but keep it in. Don't get in no trouble over nothing."

January 12, Sunday

"I just got finished f—in' this black nigger bitch in the subway," he says to me as we walk past each other in front of Lord and Taylor. It's Sunday morning early, when only street people are around. The joggers aren't out yet.

There's a guy on the street in front of the Blue Moon Saloon, and he's holding up jumper cables, waving them, as cars pass by. "Maybe I can sell them and make a couple of dollars on these," he says.

I go to a big church for Mass, but I am too late for one liturgy and too early for the other. Breakfast is being served, so I go downstairs and ask if I can have some fruit. "The cold breakfast is three dollars," the man says. "I don't have $3," I say. (I did have three dollars but it had to last until dinner). "Well the cold breakfast is $3 and the hot breakfast is $5. You'd better make up your mind because we are closing breakfast. It's time for the adult forum." "Please," I say, looking at the leftovers, "I only want some of that fruit."

I am moments from tears, moments from weeping for the whole church and for my deepest hopes for the church I love. Here I am, looking for that piece of bread and those few fish that sustained thousands. Just a piece, please. After all, they were leftovers.

I go to the adult class to hear a lesson about historic Christmas sermons. "Hello, Father," I say, "I'm coming for the lesson. I came for breakfast, but I didn't have enough money." He says distractedly, "Yes, well come to the class."

Fr. Gaiter is bright and witty, with a pair of tasteful cuff links. "The inner word is prior to language," he is quoting from something. "The inner word moans and groans to express itself." Inside me, there is a deep inexpressible word, a wound: my church is saying "no."

The lecture is excellent, but I hunger for rightness. I guess I could have begged for breakfast with tears, since I was so close to weeping for the church that I love, but true generosity must not be manipulated by imposing guilt. I listen to the lecture and read the Gospel of Luke at the same time.

Whatever house you enter, first say, "Peace to this house!" And if anyone is there who shares in peace, your peace will rest on that person; but if not, it will return to you. Remain in the same house, eating and drinking whatever they provide, for the laborer deserves to be paid. Do not move about from house to house. Whenever you enter a town and its people welcome you, eat what is set before you; cure the sick who are there, and say to them, "The kingdom of God has come near to you." But whenever you enter a town and they do not welcome you, go out into its streets and say, "Even the dust of your town that clings to our feet, we wipe off in protest against you. Yet know this: the kingdom of God has come near." Luke 10:5–11

I can't sit in the class any longer, because when the priest starts talking about the manger from which the cows ate and in which Jesus was born and how Jesus is the manger, from which we are all fed, my inner flames reach my tongue. I stand up and say, "I came for breakfast, but I did not have enough money, and so I say to you, 'The kingdom of God is near you.'" And I leave.

It's going on eleven o'clock and I still haven't been to a Eucharist. I quickly walk to another parish, and just as I enter the narthex, an usher greets me: "Good morning! Welcome! Here's a leaflet."

After I sit in a pew and say my prayers for a few minutes, a woman comes in, looking tired, even grumpy. As she slides into the pew in front of me, I say, "Good morning, my sister in Christ!" She says,

"What?" I repeat myself. Turning to me and looking me right in the eyes, she smiles, her face transformed, and says, "It is a beautiful day." I am seen and welcomed, and tears well up in my eyes. When the procession comes in, the parish priest looks at me for several seconds. He does not recognize me, but he looks at me.

When the liturgy begins, the woman in front of me turns and asks if I have a leaflet. She says, "Here take mine," but then I find mine under my jacket.

I feel like taking off my shoes, for I have found sacred ground here. I am being washed by the beauty of worship and the broken bread. A whole loaf, broken; now there is enough for everyone, even for me.

The coffee hour might as well be renamed the members club. It's important for people who know each other to reconnect, but visitors and newcomers, or those who are a little different, discover a warm welcome upstairs that gets lost over coffee and cookies downstairs.

When you know that you're an outsider, the coffee hour only affirms your distinction. But I suppose I could be a member and still feel alone during the coffee hour; that must be even worse.

A woman at the coffee hour is selling nuts for four dollars a bag to help a charity in Africa. She comes to me and gives me a bag. I am overcome by her generosity, and I offer thanks for her gift. I have budgeted $3 for breakfast and lunch. So after all the aggravation and grace, I have lunch at the Terminal Market. It is a coffee ice cream soda for $3.50.

I return to the shelter. Maxine, Shirley, and most of the others are in the community room when I arrive at around 3 p.m. I tell them what I experienced at the church breakfast and ask, "What do you think?" "They ain't got the message," one says. Then I pull out the nuts from my jacket. "Howd'ya get the nuts in?" they ask. "I just put them in the pocket inside my jacket." "Aly, you is sumpin'," says Maxine. "You sure know how to sneak things in, cause you ain't allowed that kind of food in here." I open the bag and spread the nuts on the table.

We begin talking about money and hair, and we decide that Shirley will braid my hair for a couple of bucks. That will cut into tomorrow's meals, but I can hide some of tonight's food for tomorrow.

Later Maxine takes orders for food from Wawa's, a food convenience store, and we go together. Max has figured out how to put it in a pouch and sneak it into the shelter. I have no more food money, and someone gives me a few chips because I shared the nuts.

Shirley finishes my braids. Ouch! They are tight. My hair feels as if it will fall out. It looks real good, though, like when I had chemo and was bald.

A couple of hours later, Shirley comes up to me and asks, "Are you mixed?" "I don't think so," I reply. "Well, you ain't got white girl's hair. You can't braid them white girls; their hair don't work. You're mixed, Aly; you got good hair." "Well, I might be," I say, "maybe a long time ago." Shirley laughs and smiles, "Yeah, you sure is mixed."

I remember 1981, and the following six years that I spent in a small inner-city mission. The doorbell rang all day long with people looking for food. We had no secretary or sexton, leaving me solely responsible for answering the many people who sought help. Most of the time, I didn't have anything to give. Sometimes I was so tired and frustrated; I did not act with kindness. We are all subject to a variety of moods and levels of generosity and patience. I can understand why a church refuses to give food away. They may not be able to respond to all the requests. I may understand, yet I am troubled. I do not have answers, only deep pain at being part of a society that does not care for its poorer members.

January 13, Monday

I am very compelled by the project, this pilgrimage to my soul. It began by needing to be fed by the poor, and indeed I have feasted at the holy manger of the grace and generosity of the homeless and from churches. But the unexpected has slipped in: the judgmental glances and isolation that I experienced in several churches across denominations.

I finally understand the power of the Crucifixion. The crowd really didn't like Jesus, and Peter was really scared. The man we portray as going after the one lost sheep is also the man who gives the hard parables that we like to think are meant for someone else.

The loving Jesus did not come with Band-Aids and antibacterial ointment; he came as God's word, and the healing balm was painful truth, and the promise was that out of this truth we would be set free. But truth is vague today. We even change the definition of words to distort their meaning. The president and his advisors re-define "torture" so that the horrific treatment inflicted upon prisoners is judged as acceptable.

I was tired with a pablum Jesus before I entered my pilgrimage. The pastoral ministry often sacrifices the painful road to personal transformation in order to maintain a false sense of contentment. In striving to keep people "happy" and appease dissatisfaction, we sacrifice the power of the Cross. Entering the absolute poverty of Jesus' rejection, loneliness, and eventual death is the only way to experience his Resurrection. Unless we identify with the crowd that cries, "Crucify him. Crucify him," we have yet to claim the fear and anger, envy and sloth that dwell within us. Failure to admit our participation in perpetuating the plight of the poor and rejected inhibits us from receiving the freedom and new life that we desperately seek. I know that if humanity is to inherit the kingdom of God, it will be because the poor have opened the door.

At the Eliza Shirley shelter in Philadelphia the curfew is late: 10:30 during the week. They come on the loud speaker at 10 or 11 p.m. and everyone has to do chores. We get to bed around midnight. No matter where I go, noise is part of the cultural landscape. Loud voices, loud TV, lights on almost all night, if not in the room then in the hallway.

I'm so glad I found my earplugs. One night at Welcome Arthur, Kathy saw them on my bed. They are small, green, and made of sponge. She asked what they were, and when I told her, she said she wished she had some, so I gave her my spare pair.

The list at one shelter includes, "no cursing" but there's so much use of foul language that it's an impossible rule to enforce. There's rarely a sentence without an expletive. In fact, cursing hardly seems wrong anymore.

Every shelter has its rules, its written boundaries, so we can live together with some degree of safety and respect. At Welcome Arthur, once you're in you're in. The bus drops you off at 5:30 p.m., and except for a brief cigarette break at 8:30 p.m., that's it. Lights are out by 9 p.m. At Welcome Arthur, if you're not in by 5:30, chances are there won't be a bed in cold weather.

YOU MUST HAVE SUMPIN' GOOD

January 14, Tuesday

I'm reading the Gospel of Matthew straight through. It's fast, compelling, and challenging; Jesus is on the move: healing, changing, and transforming. We're all indicted by the message, all given hope. Parables open our eyes: though our eyes may sting, we have the opportunity for real vision.

There's a guy in a car outside Crossroads. He wears the face of too much booze and cigarettes. For some reason, four firemen check his car and ask him to walk a little way down the street. He does so without issue and even does a little dance step when he turns around. One of the firemen remarks on his nimbleness, and they all laugh. They ask him to remove his car from the sidewalk.

He rolls down his window and asks a guy on the sidewalk, "Where's Maggie?" "She's downstairs." "Tell her I'll drive around the block and come back." When he returns, Maggie still hasn't arrived. He goes around the block again. Maggie and a guy come to the sidewalk and look for the car. She says, "I bet I don't even remember his f—in' name." A police car drives up and parks on the sidewalk.

Maggie and the guy walk down to the corner to wait. The fellow in the car cruises past Crossroads and on down the street, where he picks up Maggie. The guy who escorted Maggie to the corner sees her into the car and walks on. The policeman looks at me. I'm the only one left in front of Crossroads.

I go to the library. They still cannot find the fax that Pat, my case manager, sent over. I think it's a lost cause, and it may not matter anyway. The computers and periodical room are open even if I don't have a card.

I read about the governor of Illinois, Governor Ryan, commuting the death sentences for all those inmates on death row in Illinois. The article cites the number of cases where proper legal assistance was not available. I'm sitting here grateful for his courage. Surely the opposition will be great.

TOO COLD FOR WAITING

January 15, Wednesday

The weather is very cold, below freezing all day and night. The story is that every shelter is full. Welcome Arthur turned away a man last night, but there may have been a reserved bed that remained empty. This morning about a dozen of us went to city hall and then on to the *Providence Journal*'s building to raise the consciousness of the state and city to the plight of the homeless. My participation is guarded because I want to preserve my anonymity and honor the very real and capable effort of several of the clients from Crossroads. It's only 10:30 a.m., and it's already been a long day.

At 5:18 a.m. I took two buses so I could go home to change backpacks. My right arm has been affected by the one I have (I have to be careful because of previous surgery). By 7:15 a.m. I am eating breakfast at Amos House.

There are so many different people with such a variety of needs: disabled, single with children, mentally ill, capable of working, not capable of working, alcohol- or drug-dependent, drug pushers, receiving money and actively searching for a job or apartment. It would be good for clients to volunteer for chores.

At Welcome Arthur I tell the upstairs matron that if there isn't enough room for someone I'd be willing to return to Crossroads. "It don't matter. The rule is once you have a bed it's yours. That's the rule." "Even if I'm willing to leave?" "We have rules here."

A woman is yelling "Fire drill!" It's a joke, but not a funny one. The matron does nothing. She does nothing except worry about towels and the number of sheets a person takes.

"I'm not allowed to visit in the other room because there's a bitch there that I don't get along with. I know that I'm loud, but I'm trying to keep the peace. If I go in there I can get very angry."

"If you're pregnant and you have a craving for something, eat an ice cube and it will taste just like what you crave."

A woman wanders in and asks, "Where's the party?" Another answers in high spirits, "The party is in my pants and only one person's invited!"

The toilets always seem to be stopping up. I report a problem to the matron. "There's nothing we can do about it. There's no one here who can fix it." "But every night there seems to be a problem." "There's no one here to fix it." I think to myself, that's impossible. How can you have a nightly problem with the plumbing and not get it fixed?

Later, I ask, "Can you please tell me when you reported problems with the toilets?" One of the clients, who has befriended the matron/guard enters the conversation and says emphatically, "There is nothing she can do about it." I'm just wondering when an official report was made. I understand that if clients are friendly with the guard, it behooves the clients to defend the hand that feeds them or gives them some privilege.

I'm wondering who evaluates the mechanicals in the building:

> Room temperature
> Water temperature in showers
> Maintenance and cleaning
> The staff
> The rules
> Frequency of inspections

Sarah is often the guard. People seem to like her, and when I ask one of the women why, she says, "Because when Sarah's on, I'm not gonna get my ass kicked."

I'm increasingly agitated by the lack of responsibility exercised by the upstairs personnel.

There's a video camera in the room. Why? Safety, voyeurism? Who's looking? Men? Women? Is it even working? All I know is that it's right over my bed, so I can't be seen at all.

The guards watch TV all through the night. Although the TV is in the hallway, it's so loud it can be heard in all the bedrooms as well. Even when the clients are sleeping, the guards talk loudly in the hallway. How about no TV after lights go out? How about no loud voices? Impossible!

If another member of the church sins against you, go and point out the fault when the two of you are alone. If the member listens to you, you have regained that one. Matthew 18:15

The binding and unbinding of sin. We tend to read this passage as if it is addressed to an individual; here I feel it is addressed to the whole culture, and in the light of the poor I feel we are all bound up with seeing money for personal use instead of as a tool, a commodity, a way of ensuring a better life for all people. That's the sin we're bound to, and the unbinding of that sin demands a new relationship between different segments of society.

Down and Out in Providence

He said to them, "It was because you were so hard-hearted that Moses allowed you to divorce your wives, but from the beginning it was not so."

Matthew 19:8

Does marital unfaithfulness refer only to adultery, or is there an unfaithfulness that comes from a hardness of the heart? I have a feeling we are bound together for the common good, we are wedded to each other for the good of us all. Life is as though we were married to all others. Infidelity is caused by hardness of heart. We have been unfaithful to the common good.

This is social adultery. Something has happened to the promises, the civil unspoken promises that we make to each other, that are part of a nation's moral fabric. The promises speak of our willingness to put at the disposal of the whole of society the economic and material riches of the privileged few.

I am overwhelmed by reading the whole of Matthew at once. It's swift, and exciting, with Jesus doing, saying, and challenging. Of course crowds followed him because he was giving out food, wisdom, and healing. But how many really wanted to adhere to his message? Maybe that's why Jesus often told his disciples not to tell anyone what they had seen or heard. Jesus could give out free cigarettes here, and everyone would come, but they might miss the message.

ONCE A WRITER

January 15

Priscilla wanders into the room with her towel swinging by her side. She places her sheet on her bed, as is her habit, and says to no one in particular, "You do not force people who are tired to have sex on the street." She continues, "If I don't have enough freedom in my life I have no love, no joy, no sex. If I haven't got freedom I can't live right."

Priscilla says she wrote about integration for eleven years, and now she worries about freedom. Her parents had a housekeeper named Laura Mae. Priscilla says she had a daughter named Laura. I wonder what kind of life Priscilla led. Priscilla who? What is her last name? Did she publish? "They were angry with me, very angry. All the people who seem kind, but not when it comes to integration. I was always for integration; that's why they were angry with me." Priscilla makes her bed very carefully, with her sheet properly tucked under the mattress. She doesn't want anyone to help her; she does it the way she wants to do it. Without saying another word, she pulls the blanket up over her head and starts giggling.

January 16

The next day I have to pick up a prescription from the pharmacy, so I take an early bus that drops teenagers at a local high school. After picking up my prescription, I return on the next bus. When we stop at the high school, three students get on. There has been a fire drill, and they have decided to take off the rest of the day. I think student bus passes should be honored only before and after school hours and not in the middle of the day, except for school-approved emergencies.

I wish that I could invite some of these students to the shelter. They need to know now what lies ahead. I want to invite them to a friendly church, where people will welcome them and love them and give them opportunities they never had before.

The bus drops me off at Kennedy Plaza and I return to Crossroads, where a new man enters the community room.

THE TRICKLE-UP EFFECT

January 16, Morning

Six and a half years ago, Joe fell from scaffolding on the site where he was an engineer. His lawsuit is still tied up in the courts. "I got involved with a younger woman, and when our child was six months old, she left me. So I raised my daughter myself." Then, when his daughter was eleven years old, she died of meningitis, and Joe also lost his house.

"What do I have to live for? I took drugs and drank and they picked me up and put me in SSTAR. I woke up there. So now I'm here, and I'm goin' right back there because I don't want to touch nothin.' I want to do what's right." SSTAR is a drug rehab center.

Izzy said, "I want to show you what's in my backpack. There's an extra pair of blue jeans, socks, shampoo, small razor, pliers to fix somethin', pens, highlighters, toothpaste, three pairs of underwear and scissor for my nose hairs." He was proud of his compact collection. "On this side are my sunglasses and extra batteries, and here's my street sheet and aspirin in case I get a headache." Izzy has been living like this for two years.

The police come for the second time today. Three big guys hold a photograph. They walk through the community room and don't find who they're looking for. They did the same thing last week. "Whoever they's lookin' for must have done sumpin' really bad, 'cause them police don't give up their free time for nothin'."

A Phoenix newspaper has a very accurate article on the homeless of Rhode Island. The woman they highlight is the elegant black woman that I met in the Family Shelter. One of the women at Crossroads reads the article and tells us of her own journey to homelessness. It's a typical story of marriage, divorce, loss of home, loss of job, eviction from an apartment. She's college educated, has several job applications in the works, but hears nothing or is told she is overqualified.

I'm getting confused on the street. Are the faces I see from the church, from the art world, from

Crossroads or from another shelter? I wonder if I will ever be able to make a difference with this population.

⌒

It's difficult to know how to "come out" to the folks at Crossroads and Welcome Arthur. Some will be upset, others, hopefully, supportive. I've really grown to love these folks and I don't want to cause any more pain and suffering than they are already experiencing.

So many people serve us while they make almost nothing in their low-paying jobs. They lose work because of corporate greed and compromises made in the interest of profit. Low-income workers live on the edge. I wonder who exactly are the low-income workers? They say a living wage in Rhode Island is $10.19 an hour, but who can live on that? So I guess low-income workers are people who don't earn at least $11 an hour.

Children's faces show the exhaustion of always being on the move. They can feel the fragility of their parents and the hostility of other adults.

I'm writing at a table in the mall, where everything is on sale and very enticing. Our whole economy is based on consumption. It seems the trickle-down effect hasn't worked. Maybe it's time to try the trickle-up effect. Give to the poor what they need and allow the economy to respond. Allow the poor to satisfy their basic needs of shelter, clothing, and food.

January 16, Evening

It's gallery night and all the art galleries are open. Nancy said that the arcade served free food. The wraps by the Japanese shop are delicious. So is the cheese and chicken and vegetable quesadilla. Now I'm drinking peppermint tea that I bought for one dollar and eating a chocolate chip cookie form the Providence Cookie Company. That was fun.

One of the galleries has gloomy human figures made out of wooden pieces, floor nails, and just about anything that looks old and dusty. I can identify most of the objects that were used in the work to develop the characters, and I find the materials intriguing, but the art is not something to look at every day.

My Nakashima bench comes to mind. I don't need it, and it's worth a lot. Should I keep such a beautiful piece of artwork, or should I sell it and give the proceeds to those who have no bench, or bed? How am I going to free myself from my possessions? Traveling light has made me swift-footed and has given me time to live more fully in the present. No bag, no purse, one pair of sandals. Jesus knew something. (Later, I sold the bench.)

There is no stress for me here, save seeking food and shelter, which is possible to find, but it takes time and energy. Here and now, I'm not responsible for anything, but it's only because I'm the bishop that people give me the authority to speak in the press. It is an expensive price to pay.

So many people work just to provide for their needs. There's little joy and not much opportunity for creative contributions. They're just able to make it through the week until the weekend comes. Variety and some level of choice are gifts in my ministry, but I've never known what it's like to have two predictable days off. No matter what you do in life there are trade-offs.

January 17. Friday

It's 6:45 a.m. The morning starts with an argument. John is sleeping at a table where Carl sits. Chris comes in and says, "Wake up, John, and get outta my chair." Carl likes his spot at the end of the table where he can rest his back against the wall. The sense is that John is intruding in Carl's space, even though John is upset at having been awakened and yelled at. Carl makes it into his chair without incident. The security guard speaks to both guys, but he sides against John almost immediately, and so do the people at the table. "Carl only said 'good morning,'" they testify to the guard. "He didn't do nothin'." The guard heats up Carl's sandwich in the microwave. John leaves.

With a hand raised above her head and a smile on her face, Hilda says, "I'm going to school today; Katherine Gibbs. I'm going to work in an office!" "You ain't wearin' those slippers," the guard replies. "No, but I need a pair of socks." "I'll get you some socks," says the security officer.

Bill comes in with canned peaches in a Styrofoam bowl. He spills the syrup as he moves, and the guy behind him walks through it, followed by many other pairs of feet. Soon we're all sticking to the floor.

John returns. A guy named Alex says, "Let it go, man," Carl slaps John on the back and they shake hands.

Tomorrow, Saturday, I'm taking the bus to Boston to go to Gayle Harris's Ordination and Consecration to the Episcopate in the Diocese of Massachusetts. I'll know a lot of people in attendance, but I'm not worried. My "look" has gone unrecognized wherever I've been, and the same will happen tomorrow.

January 18, Saturday

The guard at the Welcome Arthur shelter told us last night that the bus will come at 5:19 a.m., even though the schedule downstairs says Saturday, 5:48 a.m. So three of us wake up at about 4:20 a.m. Linda and Sarah get dressed and go outside for a cigarette.

I take my braids out because my head is killing me. My hair is very curly. "Hello," says Wanda in her deep morning voice. It is the first time she has said hello to me since she accused me of butting into her business. A group was watching TV and she had said to us that her boyfriend had bought a car and that he'd have to pay fifty dollars a week for fifty-two weeks. She wanted a pen to figure out how much it would cost. So I said, "I think it's $2,600." "I wasn't f—in' talkin' to you!" she yelled. That was about two weeks ago, and now she's finally talking to me.

I go downstairs about twenty minutes later, and the new guard on duty says that the bus isn't due until 5:48 a.m. "It's right on the schedule. Just read it." I ask, "Can I go outside and tell them the bus isn't coming until 5:48 a.m.?" "Once you're out, you're out. Can't come back in," he replies. It is a wickedly cold morning, so through the glass in the door, I mouth, "The bus; 5:48 a.m.!"

When I go to the bus stop at 5:20 a.m. or so, Linda is crying from a pain in her leg. She is frail and hardly able to stand. For a moment I think that I won't give her my sleeping bag liner because it has just been washed, and I don't want it to get dirty in the mud. I am repelled by these thoughts. I pull out the fleece liner and put it around her shoulders and take off my jacket and wrap it around her legs. My arms ache from holding her, but I am strangely aware of how warm I am.

Florence and Wanda come to the stop and take off their jackets and hold up Linda, who is shaking with cold and in great pain. The bus arrives about ten minutes later. When we arrive in Providence, I run to get help at Crossroads, and Florence and

A Journal of Days

Wanda carry Linda to the building. We get Linda downstairs, in a chair, and wrapped in Kathy's quilt. Florence and Kathy will watch with her during the day, and I'll get permission from the social worker to stay at Crossroads with her tonight.

A couple of days later we will learn that some of the metal pins in Linda's leg had snapped. I will also learn that my already injured left bicep tendon has torn. It was only about 35 degrees on that horrible morning when we waited for the 5:48 a.m. bus.

I just caught the bus to Boston for the ordination. I open my Bible, and this is what is before me:

> *I came that they may have life and have it abundantly.*
>
> *He that doeth the will of God abideth forever.*
>
> *And the word was made flesh and dwelt among us.*
>
> *Seek ye first the kingdom of God and his righteousness.*
>
> *He that loveth not, knoweth not God, for God is Love. KJV*

Always the clear focus.

Gail Harris will be ordained and consecrated at Trinity Church in Copley Square at 11 a.m. If I'm there by 9 a.m. or 9:30 a.m., I should be able to get a seat. I make it in time. It's four and a half hours after Linda and the bus stop. Most of the pews are reserved for specific groups. It makes sense to reserve seats for those in the choir, in processions, or in the immediate family. But for other groups? I thought we were all part of the baptized.

Over the years, Drew, Jim, Alfredo, Tom, Barbara, Bud, Doug, Chilton, Arthur, and today Gail, are my sister and brother bishops whom I pray for today and with whom I rejoice in knowing that we share in Christ's servanthood. Together we go forth to proclaim the gospel, and we are misunderstood, overly praised, hit with the spit of projection, and entrusted to be models of Jesus himself. It is a vocation that rends as much as it mends, and it has the power to heal in the very heart of our woundedness.

Through words and windows, murals and sculpture, the building is a vessel in waiting. All morning people fill the vessel: musicians, clergy, invited guests. The church should always be singing a new song to God.

A Journal of Days

Come, let us sing to the Lord,
Let us shout for joy
To the rock of our salvation.

Linda keeps coming to mind, her vulnerability, her pain, her powerlessness. There was no way to get the guard to open the door this morning. I understand the importance of rules, but I think of how often mercy and compassion have been abused. Only wise, very wise, people can maintain the balance between rigidity and relaxation, between honoring the need for laws and boundaries and knowing how and when to take the great risk of crossing thresholds. After all, people want the rules to be the same for everyone, except when they have a special need. Ah, how to be fair and even handed, and fair and unevenhanded, for the sake of compassion. We would all have understood if the guard had made an exception this morning. Our collective wisdom would have welcomed an uneven response.

Today Linda, a woman of few words, had many tears; she had intense pain, she may have been embarrassed, she may have felt the whole weight of her hard and difficult life. I like to think that she also felt our common bonds of deep affection and survival, that we were and would be there for each other: today was her day. We were a few people standing at a bus stop before the break of day, sheltering each other against the natural and the systemic chill of life.

The liturgy weaves its way in spite of my reflection on the early morning. The preacher is into his sermon, and he quotes a nineteenth-century priest: "No man can say what mysteries are yet to unfold."

I am thinking that when we strive only for symmetry, we miss many things. Things that are asymmetrical are full of leaps and setbacks.

I've been on a pilgrimage, and here I am at Trinity Church, at Gail Harris' ordination, and the Gospel reading for the day is Jesus asking Peter: "Do you love me? Do you love me?" Again and again, Jesus defines love through action. "Feed my sheep." "Tend my sheep."

I am on a journey and here is Jesus in word and song, in ancient liturgy and fresh expression, in the ministry I share with my sister and brother bishops. I am so proud of them, adorned in the beauty of ceremonial garments, while my heart knows the vulnerability and nakedness that wraps us in tears.

Linda, in the morning, in the dark and cold before daybreak, stood at the bus stop and Jesus' love was revealed in the giving of jackets and blankets, in words of hope, but not too many words, with the giving of backs to lean against, and knees, and bodies to block the cold, biting wind.

I am to bring good news to the poor, yet they have brought good news to me. They have opened my eyes and set me free. And all this has visited me today: Linda's suffering and the self-giving of those gathered around her, Gail's ordination and the coming together of the baptized. We all struggle and we take off our jackets and blankets, wrapping each other in the warmth of sacrificial love. We are all Linda, and we are all Jesus, and we can know our completeness: God completed the creation in us.

Behind me, three seminarians from an ecumenical theological school are complaining about the procession and the way the bishops are vested. I am very upset, not so much with their comments, but that they are making so much noise. I turn around and say to them, "May the solemnity of the occasion overcome your judgment with joy."

The ushers are gesturing us to receive communion. Here there will always be enough. And I hunger, and I thirst. It is a marvelous thing to hunger and thirst: it leads to fresh springs and rejoicing.

Some people say it is bishops who should speak truth to those in power, but the poor have a spiritual power whose truths I am still learning.

I choose not to go to the reception, even though I know it will offer free food and drink. I take the next bus back to Providence.

⌒

I get to the Church of Epiphany meal site just before closing. My heart leaps when I see one of my priests and his people working at the meal site. I'm so proud of our churches. They even give me some food to take back to Linda, and when I see her back at Crossroads we hug and weep. Her gratitude drowns me in love. "Love isn't huggin' and kissin'," she says, "it's taking off your jacket in the cold weather, and Wanda lettin' me sit on her, and it's Florence keepin' me warm, and that girl givin' me her coat, and Wanda just about carryin' me to the elevator. God, I'll never forget any of ya. That's what love is."

People say we should pull ourselves up by our bootstraps, but these folks who may not have boot-straps or other resources can pull you up by their sheer guts and integrity.

Even without her front teeth, Linda eats the sandwich from the meal site with joy and thanks-giving. Someday I will tell the people at that church what they meant to a woman they have never met.

At 5:30 p.m. Crossroads reminds us that we will all have to be out by 6 p.m. I pick up my backpack and go to Kennedy Plaza to wait for the 22 bus to Welcome Arthur. "I'll give you ten f—in' sec-onds to get out of here!" yells a large woman to a guy at the other end of the waiting area. "5, 4, 3, 2. You got one second left, bastard!" By that time the guy has hopped into a car across the street. "Didn't I tell ya he'd get outta here," she says with a triumphant grin, while playfully slapping the guy standing next to her. She keeps pointing her fingers and mouthing off, threatening to report the secu-rity guard to his supervisor for not treating her right. "What's your badge number? I want to see your badge number. I'm gonna report you." The security guard moves closer to her and doesn't say a thing. I look; it's badge #14. The security guard is no saint, but no saint could have done better with the loud woman.

I recognize the woman; she stays at Welcome Arthur, the shelter. Two of her children are Cosmos, eleven, and David, six or seven. Sensitive David, his anger and behavior problems increase day by day. I, too, am angry at the fat, hard-drinking, out-of-control, loud-mouthed woman who slaps David and whose fierce tongue lashes out at random targets. Her actions burn hot against everything she touches.

January 19, Sunday

One of the old-timers at Crossroads is grumbling about the shelter and about people who want everything for nothing. I ask him, "So what would you do if you ran a shelter?" "First, if you get a check from SSI for six hundred dollars, you give all but one hundred dollars to the shelter. Maybe ya get twenty-five dollars a week or a hundred dollars all at once. If you've got money for alcohol, you got money to get out of here. And I'll tell you something else: if you come into the shelter smellin' of alcohol, that's it, you're out. You're a scum on the street. You're allowed to live in the shelter for six months. That gives you time to save your money and get an apartment."

Carl joins the conversation. "I ain't getting an apartment anyway, because I killed two people and have one armed robbery. I ain't going nowhere. I got one major problem: my temper. I also have fifty-two felons and they won't erase them without a lawyer, and I ain't getting a lawyer."

Jim calls out, "I got felons too. All for drugs, though. That ain't as bad as murder."

Jim is about six foot five and has a huge frame. The more he talks, the more his tales become pre-posterous. After a half hour his stories are so off that none of the other guys try to outdo his tales of violence.

A woman asks me, "When a woman rolls you [hits you], whudd ya gonna do?" "I'd probably walk away," I say. "You ain't gonna defend yisself? Come on. Yes or no? Ya gonna stand up?" "I'd probably just walk away," I say again, "because I'm not that strong, and nothing would come from fighting anyway." She keeps on provoking me until I finally say, "Yeah, probably I'd fight back." She smiles and leaves me alone.

It's part of the culture, the "jungle" as Chris calls it. You have to keep your mouth shut most of the time and know when to talk and when not to.

An announcement is made to the effect that all people who have a home or who have relatives to go to are to leave Crossroads because the room is over crowded and a safety hazard. People grumble and most stay.

When an announcement like that is made, people need time to react. With this group the first reaction is anger, then griping, then brave statements: "We're marchin' on city hall!" "We're goin' to the *Providence Journal* !" When I suggest we go to one of the nearby churches to make our point of needing more shelters, Christine reacts immediately. "We ain't goin to no church!" she yells.

My thought is that if twenty people went to each of the seven or so churches in the immediate area, we would have a more long-term effect. After all, seven churches, especially at ten in the morning, are going to wonder why so many homeless people are attending church when it's only 3 degrees outside. Then we could tell our story. No one liked the idea.

In the community room, many people have swift reactions, almost a sense of retaliation, but there is not much sense of process or planning.

One of the problems at Crossroads is mixed signals. A security person came into the room and made the announcement about leaving if you have somewhere to go. It was also announced on a PA system. Then a police officer came into the room and went to a man sleeping at the first table. I don't know why, but other guys began making comments. So the police officer let the first guy go and went toward another guy. The officer then announced that everyone was to leave the room so they could wash the floor.

I said to the police officer, very politely, "Are you asking everyone to leave because the floor is going to be washed or because there are too many people here?" "You'll have to ask them," he said, pointing to the front desk. I asked the guy at the desk. He also gave out mixed messages. He said the floor was going to be washed, but moments later, when the desk woman returned, she said people had to leave because of overcrowding, nothing about the floor being washed.

Down and Out in Providence

Tabitha, one of the guards at Welcome Arthur, invites me to her church, whose name she can't remember. Actually, there are three churches in one building. When I arrive I go upstairs to the Methodist service. The final strains of "Glorious Things of Thee Are Spoken" is being enthusiastically sung by a small, racially mixed congregation.

The minister greets me at the door with more than a perfunctory hello. After responding to her question, "Are you from the neighborhood?" we get to discussing the housing and homeless situation in Providence. The United Methodist churches are gathering together to figure out what ministry to offer in the city. The minister is also learning how to speak Spanish. She expresses the need for a legislation advocate, like a lobbyist. She then shows me how to get to Shiloh Gospel Temple, Tabitha's church. It is downstairs.

Three churches all meet in the one church building at different times and places. I make my way downstairs, and it takes a while to find my way through the many halls and rooms.

The green-and-beige-striped curtains are drawn open to show the stage. Two aluminum-framed tan upholstered chairs are separated by a glass-topped chrome table. In the center a pulpit is wrapped with a pressed white sheet that has a large black cross on the front. At one time this was probably the parish hall for Washington Park United Methodist Church.

On the floor level and stage right is a piano, drums, and a sax. Metal chairs are covered with newly pressed pillow cases. Tabitha told me to come at 11 a.m., and now at noon people are just beginning to assemble. A woman in a white dress is sweeping the floor. Pastor Perry's been here for over an hour, getting everything ready. The pastor's wife is called co-pastor or first lady.

The pianist, about forty, and the teenage drummer are creatively working through various tunes. Pastor Perry has just changed from his shirt and jeans to a clerical collar, black suit, and shoes. He's helping to wire up the PA system.

An attractive woman in a white dress brings me a Holy Bible, containing the Old and New Testaments, King James Version.

"I'm so glad you're here" calls Tabitha from the rear of the room. I'm not sure where she goes after our embrace. In fact, I'm not sure where anyone is, and it's now 12:15 p.m.

I'm wondering when we're going to start, but as I look around at the women reading their Bibles, I suspect that we've already begun in some measure.

It's 12:30 p.m. and Pastor Perry is preaching: "The spirit upon you is different from the power of the spirit in you."

His message is that we have choices. Every child here should do well in school. This is a choice. You can choose to break a window or not break a window. The sermon lasts a good forty-five minutes, then there is prayer and praise. Hands are lifted, and large women dance in the aisles. The offertory is long and challenging, and the pastor is not afraid to speak of money. I leave to catch the 3:02 p.m. bus. Walking up the steps through another part of the building, I hear more music. A Hispanic congregation gathers around 1 p.m. or 2 p.m. The Shiloh Tabernacle Temple meets again at 7:30 p.m.

January 20, Martin Luther King Jr. Day

Charles says to me, "I'm waitin'. Are you gonna be my woman or not?" "Charles, I really can't. It's not

~ 130 ~

a good time." I have to lie here, or really stretch the truth: "I'm working things out with someone."

This morning I see Joe again. I remember his story. I think he's very handsome, and he thinks I'm beautiful and he would like to get to know me. I'd like to get to know him too. I find him interesting. He's the fellow who fell off the scaffolding and lost his daughter to meningitis.

One of the Crossroads employees is on the verge of tears this morning. So many people, so many problems. Crossroads is overcrowded. There are too many different needs. Emotional instability is present everywhere. Anger flares with little or no provocation. A harmless glance is construed as judgment or attack. The ownership of space, chairs and tables, creates boundaries and potential struggles for turf. Yet when you're homeless, creating a boundary for personal space can help create a sense of security that's so essential for personal safety and identity.

Food is another source of contention. A tray of cheese danish appears. Those at the end of the line usually go without because those in front take many servings and horde their food. I can understand this without condoning it. If you're not sure when food will be contributed to Crossroads, it's logical to take more than enough for yourself when it does come. Those who are strong boldly announce that they want food, and there's always someone who will give of their own. No one goes hungry; even those who are quiet are looked after.

January 21. The Feast

"Aly," asks one of the directors, "will you help Carl prepare dinner tonight?" Prepare dinner!? What could there possibly be in the kitchen to prepare; more cold pizza? "Yes, I'm happy to help," I say. "Hey, Carl," I say, walking toward the kitchen, "I'm helping you cook." His eyes light up. Carl's dream is to open a first-class 1920's-style restaurant downtown, complete with valet parking and live music.

"Okay, Aly, get out all the food; let's see what we have. I'm gonna wash all the pots. Ya can't start cookin' unless the pots are spotless." "Carl," I muse, "why don't we do a real dinner: appetizers, tablecloths, waiters and waitresses. The whole nine yards." Carl grins, his brilliant white teeth stretching across the kitchen, his eyes dancing. I go into one of the community rooms and ask, "Anyone want to volunteer to be a waiter or waitress for a special dinner that Carl and I are cooking?" Four people quickly volunteer. Wayne volunteers to be the third cook.

"Hurry up," says Carl, "everyone's hungry. Get the appetizers out." As the appetizers leave the kitchen, pork, chicken, pasta salad, asparagus, potatoes, and bread are all readied for serving.

It is fabulous. We laugh, use every pot and serving tray to be found, and bring a moment of elegance to grateful diners. A lot of food had been donated, and we made a real restaurant out of the community room.

Filled with the energy of doing a good job, we go on to strip and wax the worn green floors, wipe down all the furniture, vacuum the carpets, and clean up the kitchen. What a sense of accomplishment!

"Hey, why in the hell is the community room closed?" asks a man who had just come into Crossroads. "Because the floor is drying." "I don't care about no f—in' floor, I want to sit at my table." "Yeah, ya can wash the floor some other time, who gives a f— about the floor," adds someone else.

The group who is washing, polishing, and buffing just keep working and pulling together, talking, encouraging, teasing, and laughing.

In two hours, everything is finished, a great night! Tonight we all came alive in a new way. We may have had only leftover food to cook and eat, but tonight none of us felt like leftover people.

"Women and children should have homes." This man doesn't say much, and his comment is directed at no one in particular. "If I won a $150 million from the lottery, I'd be giving money away to help people." He goes on, warming to his subject. "People need jobs. That's what we need, a job that pays so you can get an apartment. I had a chance to win $160 million, but I didn't have the money to buy the lottery ticket." His final statement: "The rich don't want to help the poor."

January 21, Later

I'm not sure why, but Anne assembles a group of Crossroad staff members, and tells them who I am. In response to her question "How are you feeling about Bishop Wolf having been here for a month?" most have a sense that they have been deceived. They think they could have been trusted with the information. Anne is very good in expressing her own dilemma and in explaining the reasons she chose not to reveal my identity. Misgivings remain, but they trust Anne and support her.

The group expresses concern as to how I will "come out." I am concerned as to how I will leave. I've become very fond of many people and will miss the company of the group. The diversity of the population and constant conversations never cease to engage me.

Vaughn, one of the directors at Crossroads, and I talk about how I will tell people. Vaughn is a tall, attractive man of color, with a wonderful way of allowing grumbles and complaints to be expressed without feeling the need to defend the agency. I decide that I will first tell Wayne and Izzy. We have become very good friends in the shelter, and Izzy jokes about the three of us sharing an apartment. Since neither of them could marry me without hurting the other, this was the next best thing. With Wayne and Izzy still in the room, I will invite Kathy, Florence, and Bob to join us. They represent different constituencies at the shelter, and Florence is highly respected by the group as a whole. Each of them will advise me as to how to tell the larger group.

I keep thinking about what it will be like when I tell my first five homeless friends. I don't want to embarrass them in any way, or suggest that I was prying. The truth is, I'm so very fond of each one of them, and I'm very grateful for their friendship and what we have shared together.

January 22. Wednesday

"It's 71 degrees in L.A. and 3 degrees or so here," says Leah, reading the paper. Part of me doesn't want to leave these people, this place, where emotions are so mixed and basic needs are expressed with such fundamental language. There are no masks, no subtleties, but there are many robust conversations with dramatic gestures.

I feel as though I can make a difference here. I love the community, its earthiness and the gifts of hard love and easy generosity.

Last night I was put in a small room at the old YMCA, and I was lonely, all by myself. The common room there was too smoky, so was my bedroom. I didn't have the energy to make acquaintances. I missed all the chaos and the people I've grown to respect and admire.

In the Crossroads window, a sign reads:

> Preserving Dignity
> Building Independence
> Restoring Pride

Wayne is so excited. Channel 10 sent a camera crew to Crossroads, and Wayne and Kathy were interviewed. Wayne was direct and articulate. Kathy brought out her emotional side: "I just want to live with my baby." "Crossroads needs gloves, hats, scarves, and coats," said the newscaster. Within a few hours, the donations start coming in droves. Wayne and I start sorting clothes at about 3 o'clock in the afternoon.

The clothes are beautiful, many are new and clean, some even vintage or antique. We group hats, gloves, and scarves in one area, and children's things in another. Coats are sorted in one pile, jackets in another, and the sweaters are all stacked up. Socks are put in a box. All other things are left for nighttime volunteers. We are just doing the essentials.

"Hey, Wayne," I call, "check out the leather jacket with the real fur inside!" It's tan on the outside and lined with soft white fleece. "Someone's really gonna enjoy that," he replies. There's a sudden honking from the street. Wayne goes out to help a donor empty a car trunk and brings in several boxes filled with brand new sweaters, still in their plastic bags.

About eight of us eat dinner at a church off Elmwood Avenue. Before we are served, the pastor gives us a message. "Sometimes it's good to go without. Things in the past may have put you where you are today. God chooses the rulers of the world." I find myself getting very agitated with the message.

From the way he speaks, I almost think he believes it is our destiny to be here. I ask, "Do you believe that God wanted Hitler to be president of Germany?" "Yes," he answers, "I do. Not all the Jews were killed. There are still Jews in the world. Everything is God's plan." I want to keep asking questions, but Rosie jabs me in the ribs. She's hungry, and she's not interested in my questions.

We listen for about half an hour, and then a very delicious meal of meat, vegetables, and rice is served. I am given a plate to take back to Linda at Crossroads, but she has already eaten. It doesn't matter; someone else finishes the meal.

It's so cold, and there are so many looking for shelter, that we are sent to different places. I decide to spend the night at Beneficent Church, where they have opened rooms for the homeless during this freezing weather. It is 9 p.m., and I'm the first one in the room that is filled with cots and blankets, and I'm going to sleep! The cots look dangerously narrow, so I opt to sleep on a thin gym mat on the floor. At least I won't fall off that.

"Rise, shine, and give God the glory, glory!" This is how we are awakened by a chipper woman who at least has the foresight or thoughtfulness not to turn the lights on. "If you want to follow me, we have coffee and cereal at the other end of the building." My bones and muscles are sore from sleeping on the floor.

Even though it seemed warm when I went to sleep, I was cold during the night and had to sleep all curled up. My left hipbone is sore. Two other women slept in this room also. I spend some time writing in my diary, or I would have left the cold room as quickly as they, in about ten minutes! That's all it takes to use the bathroom, pack up and leave. I'm off now too.

The chair at the breakfast table feels good as I move all the parts of my body that have stiffened during the night. I look in the paper for an apartment. There are more than 250 apartments and studios advertised for rent. Of those, only 16 rent for $600 or less. The cheapest apartment is $475, unfurnished. None of the cheaper apartments includes all utilities. Five are not close enough to bus routes. There is one room for $90 per week that includes utilities. There is one room for $350 per month, including utilities.

So, I figure, if I made eight dollars an hour in a full-time job, I'd have about $1,100 a month after taxes. If I didn't have children or a car, and if I was given medical insurance, then I could make it. I could start looking for one of those apartments for $575 a month, not including furniture, heat or lights. It would be a little more than half my salary, but I could do it. Or could I? I would have to find the first month's rent, the last month's rent, and a month's security deposit. That's $1,725, just to start, before a telephone. It can't be done. I put my head down on the table and close my eyes.

Why am I keeping my eyes on the ground while I'm walking? It's because I've got only three one dollar bills in my pocket and some change. I'll even pick up pennies. Found on a piece paper in the library: *www.brm.org* Boston Rescue Mission "Home for the Homeless."

Every diocesan and church employee should be paid more than the minimum wage. They say you have to earn at least $10.19 to be able to live on what you're paid, so I don't think anyone in the diocese should earn less than $11 an hour. Of course, some churches are so short of funds that they want to hire someone at the lowest salary possible. This isn't fair, and we should have a policy that no one earns under a living wage. We talk a lot about justice, and here is an opportunity to live it out in our own environment.

January 24, Last Day

It's my last day at Crossroads, and I'm very sad. Sad to leave these wonderful people. I have come to love them, their vulnerability and resilience, their honesty and uncommon generosity — even their anger and resentment.

I meet with Anne and Linda, the social worker, and realize that I am crossing the line between client and professional, and I hesitate, anticipating the loss, the impossibility of ever again living on the other side of the community room.

Then I meet with Izzy and Wayne, my true loves, two men struggling to stay sober and sane in a world that doesn't offer them much hope. I worry about Izzy, his loneliness, his mild depression and lack of self-esteem. For these past few weeks we were a threesome. We belonged to each other, a family within a group. We hung out together, cared for one another, had a good time. When I tell them who I am, Izzy reminds me and Wayne that he always knew I was "different." Izzy pulls a small stone from his pocket and gives it to me, a sign of his love. Homeless people do not carry anything that is "extra." Everything means something. He has given me a rare and beautiful treasure, a part of his life and experience. I am deeply touched. Wayne has tears in his eyes. "Aly, I love you so much that I'm just glad that you have a home to live in."

At 11:30 a.m. or so, Bob, Florence, and Kathy join Izzy and Wayne. Bob says he recognized me when I first came, but he decided not to identify me. He let it go.

Florence is in a state of disbelief. All agree that I didn't really fit in: too articulate, nice socks, just different. They all agree that I should tell everyone in the community room. I hesitate because I worry about feelings of betrayal or deception. I ask Florence to be the MC, and she agrees. We all go to the community room, and Florence gets everyone to quiet down. "Aly has something to tell ya," she says.

As I begin to speak, one man makes angry noises, "You deceived us." But Florence says, "Shut up, let her speak." The room is absolutely silent, which is frightening in its own way. I am almost numb because of the unexpected overflow of love and acceptance coming my way.

I share why I became homeless, and I pledge my continued dedication. They ask what I have learned, and I recite the difficulties of high rents, no telephone numbers or addresses, et cetera. "But most of all," I say with real affection, "I heard more cussing than I had ever heard before, and I learned a lot about sex! I also learned that if a guy had two cigarettes, another guy was always assured of at least one. I learned about family, community life, generosity, acceptance, and love." I end and thank them.

We are all in tears, hugging, offering thanks-giving, sharing hope.

Lee wraps her arms around me, "I knew who you were from the first time you smiled. I knew you from when you had cancer and were in the newspaper." "Lee," I ask, amazed, "Why didn't you say something?" "I like to keep secrets," she says with a delicious smile, "and we're sisters, and sisters don't tell on each other. Didn't you know I knew when I gave you those looks?" "Looks!" I say, "They were looks to kill!" "Yeah," she says, "that's the way I looked. I thought you would know I knew and that I would keep the secret and that you could talk to me." She laughs when I mimic her nasty looks.

Linda and Bobby, two regulars in the community room, want me to marry them in 2004, and even Rosie shares a smile. I am overwhelmed by their pure affection and love, but not really surprised, for this is part of the generosity of the poor. Perhaps, if anything, I am surprised at my own profound sense of love for each and all of them.

"Aly, I still love you," says Carl as he enfolds me in his large and fleshy body. His hearty laugh brings a sense of joy to all.

Charles comes into the room late, and the others tell him. Though I've been told he is a rough character, he has a sweetness about him as we rehearse once again his affection for me. "I always knew you were different, Aly. There's just one thing I'd really like. You know that backpack you had when you first came?" "It's yours, Charles!"

Some think I did a good job with how I looked and fit into the group. Most agree that I was somehow different, but they liked me anyway. Now I'm part of the family: "To us you're always Aly." And I agree.

In many ways this is a beginning. There's a sense of hope; someone knows about them. One thing I know is that my new friends have energy, street smarts, survival skills, and leadership abilities. Together we can build on the relationship we've begun.

Next Thursday at 9:30 a.m. we will have a brainstorming session in the community room so we can choose one or two things that we can actually accomplish. In addition, Florence, Bob, and Wayne want to come with me to Honduras where I am going next month to learn about micro-enterprise. I say I think it is a fine idea.

EPILOGUE

Florence and Bob joined me on the trip to Honduras. Wayne had trouble coping with his life, and he went downhill for a time, making it impossible for him to go. It was very sad.

In Honduras, we learned about micro-enterprise systems, and the possibility of starting a small business. We visited several agencies, which was arranged for us before I lived with the homeless. It was an extraordinary experience. Florence was her usual helpful and articulate self. Bob turned out to be troublesome in many ways. We survived and returned to Crossroads. Thankfully, Wayne had recovered, and the community anticipated our return with a party at a neighborhood bar.

The local newspaper ran an article about my experience, and those whose pictures were included and whose comments were quoted were very proud.

Several church-related newspapers and magazines included parts of the story. A fellow by the name of Walter read about our micro-enterprise journey and volunteered to help set up a program with the homeless in Rhode Island. I formed a committee that included Wayne and Florence. By this time, Florence had passed examinations and requalified for a nurses' aid position. She moved into a halfway-type house, and since then has worked in several jobs, anticipating a move to an apartment. I hired Wayne to work for me during the summer, replacing worn-out shingles on one side of my house. He did such an excellent job that I spoke to the folks at Crossroads. They hired him to work in a new facility, where he has continued to be a highly responsible and dedicated worker.

I now serve on the board of Crossroads, and I try to contribute when I can. My real offering has come through speaking to groups and bringing a new face to homelessness. People have many negative ideas about those they call homeless, or bag ladies, or drunks. Indeed, some people use the system for all it's worth. Most, however, are honest, decent people who have few opportunities for real financial independence.

Low-income housing is a desperate necessity in our country today. So is a decent minimum wage.

It's impossible to make it when basic housing is more than half of take-home pay. Our ears perk up when we hear promises of tax reduction, and our legislatures frown when a bill for a raise in minimum wages is proposed. Something is wrong with us when those who hold jobs can't afford both a place to live and food to eat. Have we gotten so independent minded that we have forgotten the common good? Is sacrifice becoming a lost word in a world of consumerism? As Christians, we listen to the story of Jesus Christ's death and resurrection, but we forget that we are called to share in this paschal mystery. We are called to sacrifice so that we and others will receive the gift of hope. Gandhi said, "Live simply so that others may simply live."

Holy Scripture bids us to live responsible lives and to give to the poor. One way we can do this is by living the biblical mandate of the tithe. Giving 10 percent of one's income for the benefit of others is a way of living below one's means. Many years ago, one of my parishioners shared that she earned $162 a week at her job, and she received about $300 a month from Social Security. She was proud to announce that she gave $100 a month to the church for its witness and ministry. "I've never been in want," she added. What a testimony to sacrifice. It's time that more of us take her experience to heart and make it our own.

To my sister and brother clergy in our various houses of worship, I know how hard you labor to live a life rooted in the best precepts of our various traditions. From my own experience of living and serving as a priest for fifteen years in the inner city, I know it can be both rewarding and grueling. At times, a decision not to serve people breakfast may have to be made. After all, when word gets out that there is free food, it is easy to be inundated with more people than can be served. My telling of experiences in our churches was not to pass judgment, but to encourage the welcome of the stranger and the person who is different.

In the past couple of years, the media has spoken loudly about homosexual rights, same-sex marriages, and the sexualization of our culture through magazines and television, quoting scripture in defense of their position. Why, I ask, do we not have the same energy for the poor? Surely, Christ's message is clear and consistent: what we do for the least of our sisters and brothers, we do for him.

It is time for us to look seriously at systemic changes to help the poor and disenfranchised. Why do we grumble when we speak of national health insurance? Why do otherwise thoughtful people complain when a home for children or the mentally ill is to be located in their neighborhood? There is nothing to fear. When politicians speak of moral values, listen to their examples. Do they match yours? Do they include sacrifice and generosity, a sincere willingness to help the millions of people without adequate housing, or the millions of children who live below the poverty line?

Though our various religious communities differ in worship and beliefs, we must redouble our efforts in addressing the needs of the poor and in working for systemic legislative changes. No working mothers or fathers in this country should have to live in a shelter with their family. No mentally ill people should spend their days bowed down in despair. No addictive persons who want help should be deprived of a chance to leave their addictions behind.

I hope that you have learned something from this book. Pass it on to someone else, and buy another copy. Every bit of profit that I receive will go to help the needy. Every time I receive an honorarium for talking about the homeless, it returns to them. Everyone who helps the poor becomes rich. To all my friends at Crossroads, I give special thanks for making me rich indeed. For a brief moment, I was dancing, and they were all watching.

ACKNOWLEDGMENTS

"Jesus meets you at the crossroads where
your life takes shape."
— Jean Lafrance

Life has many crossroads where experiences and insights intersect. Usually there is a stop sign or traffic light, a warning against oncoming traffic and potential accidents.

Few of us can maneuver through crossroads without the guidance of those who traveled successfully through the intersections of life. I'm grateful to the many people whose actions, insights, and encouragement gave strength and purpose to *Down and Out in Providence.*

I am especially grateful to the homeless people with whom I shared shelters and meals. Their stories were both heart-wrenching and life-giving, as I hope you will have discovered.

Anne Nolan and Noreen Shawcross were guiding lights throughout the days of my homeless experience. They are passionate and tireless workers on behalf of the homeless. The gifts they offer to clients and the state of Rhode Island can not be numbered. The staff that supports the programs and shelters for the homeless serve with great dedication and little thanks or remuneration. Special appreciation goes to Crossroads, Welcome Arthur, Eliza Shirley, Amos House, and all the places that serve the needs of the poor and homeless. I also thank Annette Cox, my secretary of many years, whose support and confidentiality helped enormously in the planning stages and upon my return.

Christina Rees came all the way from England to help with a first draft and to find a publisher. My Thursday night leadership group grilled me as to the purposes of living as a homeless person, and kept me honest regarding motivations and responsibilities. Fortunately Cynthia Shattuck, now at Church Publishing, was able to prove the reality of six degrees of separation by mentioning the project to Roy M. Carlisle, senior editor and an Episcopalian, no less, at the Crossroad Publishing Company who guided me and the manuscript through the publishing process with quiet determination and whose team supported the content of the original journal and pushed me to make it accessible to readers. Shirley Coe provided eye-opening guidance on grammar and phrasing for which I will always be grateful. Thank you to all who participated in the shaping of this book.

I want to express my gratitude to the Diocese of Rhode Island for giving me the opportunity to take a sabbatical. Especially, I thank those who serve in our churches and church agencies. Very few know how stressful it is to respond to the many requests made of the church. It is painful to turn away anyone because there is no more to give, save a listening ear and a prayer. At a time when social services are being cut for the neediest of our society, clergy and people of every faith are challenged to stretch resources beyond their limits.

To everyone who is willing to touch the homelessness in themselves, and thus touch the homelessness in others, my sincere and grateful thanks.

ABOUT THE AUTHOR

Geralyn Wolf is the bishop of the Diocese of Rhode Island. She is one of fourteen women bishops in the worldwide Anglican Communion. Prior to her election as bishop in 1995, she served in both mainline and urban churches in Philadelphia and was dean of Christ Church Cathedral in Louisville.

Bishop Wolf has had many and varied experiences in the church, and has a special devotion to the religious life as expressed through the monastic tradition. Prior to attending seminary she was a high school teacher and coach. For diversion, she makes whimsical wood constructions from found objects. In her artist's statement, she says, "Other people's trash becomes the raw material from which I make my figures. Most people want to throw away the painful memories of life. I believe God uses those memories as raw materials to reshape our lives."

A WORD FROM
THE EDITOR

Degrees of separation? In this case I think it should be degrees of connection. First it was many years of working with Jim Wallis on books about poverty and homelessness, spirituality and faith, which raised my consciousness. This was a more difficult journey than I had anticipated because I wanted to forget my own humble roots. Then it was my journey into the Episcopal Church, which became a spiritual "home" for me. Eventually these issues around peace and justice in the Episcopal Church became more real to me with help from friends like Tony Petrotta (my daily running partner and a priest), Walker Smith (my mentor in diverse ways around diabetes, marketing, and traditional Episcopal values), Carter Echols (who is a brilliant peace and justice organizer for the Episcopal Church), and others. Then it was the fortuitous meeting with Cynthia Shattuck, one of the truly remarkable editors in our world of Episcopal publishing, which finally led to the little journal by Bishop Geralyn Wolf.

I was literally struck mute by this powerful and compelling journey into homelessness by the bishop of Rhode Island. The courage it took was evident, the insights gleaned were numerous, but it was Bishop Wolf's reflection on that journey and how we treat "the least of these" that made this book something more than a personal journal. I cannot see the world the same way as I have in the past. I cannot avoid the heartbreak of homelessness as I have in the past. I cannot objectify homeless people in order to dismiss them as I have in the past. My sins were vividly apparent to me even if they weren't to others.

Those words might indicate that this journal increased my guilt. Not so. It was about a new vision, not about feeling badly. It was about facing new feelings of hope. This is the gift that Bishop Wolf has given all of us through her simple but profound words. We can have hope because there are people whose ministry is to run a shelter, there are people whose love is big enough to embrace a broad spectrum of struggling souls. And we are all a part of one another in the faith. So my heart was enlarged, as yours will be, by reading this book.

It is my job as an editor to take the measure of a writer. I must assess whether any particular writer has a message that is really worthy of a book-length treatment. So I am assessing character as much or more than I am deciding on whether a specific manuscript is well written and worthy of publication. Never was that task more easily accomplished than in this case. Bishop Geralyn Wolf is a woman whose life and message are inexorably intertwined in a way that enlivens faith. I am one of those whose life has been so touched. I pray that you will also meet this woman of faith in these pages and have your life touched.

ROY M. CARLISLE
Senior Editor

Of Related Interest

Joy Carroll Wallis
THE WOMAN BEHIND THE COLLAR
The Pioneering Journey of an Episcopal Priest

Foreword by Dr. Rowan Williams,
Archbishop of Canterbury

Joy's story, from wild youth, to unexpected calling to the ministry and prominent involvement in the struggle for the ordination of women, as well as a "tabloid" wedding to noted American author, activist, speaker, and professor Jim Wallis make it unsurprising that Joy Carroll was chosen as the inspiration for the acclaimed television series *The Vicar of Dibley*. This is an insightful and humorous chronicle of Joy's demanding life as a priest, wife, mother, and transplanted Brit.

0-8245-2265-6, $19.95 paperback

Please support your local bookstore,
or call 1-800-707-0670 for Customer Service.

For a free catalog, write us at

THE CROSSROAD PUBLISHING COMPANY
16 Penn Plaza, 481 Eighth Avenue
New York, NY 10001

Visit our website at
www.crossroadpublishing.com
All prices subject to change.

crossroad